W9-DGT-175

ART OF LITHUANIAN COOKING

ART OF LITHUANIAN COOKING

MARIA GIEYSZTOR DE GORGEY

HIPPOCRENE BOOKS, INC.

New York

TX
723.5
.L8
G54
1998

Copyright © 1998 by Maria Gieysztor de Gorgey

All rights reserved.

Cataloging-in-Publication Data available from the Library of Congress.

ISBN 0-7818-0610-0

For information, address:
HIPPOCRENE BOOKS, INC.
171 Madison Avenue
New York, NY 10016

Printed in the United States of America.

TABLE OF CONTENTS

# INTRODUCTION

The purpose of this book is to make available in English, and thus to preserve, a selection of recipes representative of the culinary culture of Lithuania. The book, of course, is not a historical treatise, but rather includes those recipes which—in the author's judgment—retain a practical interest at the present time. Because of the complicated network of influences, borrowings, adaptations and independent inventions of similar dishes throughout the centuries, the originality of the rich variety of ethnic culinary contributions is often difficult to judge. Many people would be greatly surprised by the claim of some historians of culture that spaghetti, this epitome of Italian cuisine, was actually invented in China to feed the workers building the Great Wall of China, or that some dishes generally considered distinctly French, in fact originated in Italy. Kolduny (see p. 83), seen by most Lithuanians and Poles as a typically Lithuanian contribution to the world's cuisine, were—according to some writers—in fact invented by the Tartars, who brought them to Northeastern Europe at the time of the Tartar invasions.

Lithuania emerged as an independent state in the middle of the thirteenth century. From 1386, when the Lithuanian Prince Jagiello became the King of Poland, until almost the end of the eighteenth century, when it was partitioned by Russia, Prussia and Austria, the Polish-Lithuanian Commonwealth played an important role in European history. For a time, it was one of the largest European powers and extended from the Baltic to the Black Sea. It included a variety of national cultures, and for most of its history was distinguished by religious tolerance, which made it attractive to people who were escaping from persecution or expelled— as the Jews—from Western European countries. This cultural variety and subsequent assimilation and interpenetration of

1

multiple ethnic traditions, Lithuanian, Ruthenian, Ukrainian, Polish, German and Jewish, is naturally reflected also in the cooking habits and preferences of the entire region. Many of these traditions survived more than a century of the Lithuanian and Polish struggle for national independence which was finally achieved at the end of World War I. During World War II, Lithuania proper was forced by the Soviet Union to become one of the Soviet Republics, and was finally liberated with the fall of the Communist empire. The "Old Lithuanian Cuisine" represented in this book is based in part on family traditions and in part on some, often quite old, literature on the subject.

The author, whose family also inhabited this part of Europe for centuries, has known most of these dishes from childhood, and has selected those recipes which seem to be original and characteristic of this region of Europe and which—in her opinion—deserve to be preserved. The choice is naturally quite subjective. Most recipes included in this book are also slightly "modernized," either because not all the materials required by the very old recipes are easily obtainable today, or because many of them, for self-evident reasons, do not pay heed to modern nutritional requirements. Making soup stock from "scratch," for instance, is very time-consuming, while we now have convenient and acceptable ready broths.

The book is intended to be practical, and not a study of purely historical interest. Thus, I did not include the notorious culinary extravagances of the Lithuanian and Polish magnates of a bygone era, such as roast boar's head, or turkey garnished with two dozen roast field thrushes. Nor will you find a recipe for peacocks, "highly prized because they are so rare," which begins with a note: "at royal banquets, a favorite dish was a pâté made of peacocks' brains, and two to three thousand birds had to be slaughtered at one time . . ."

Instead, the book will focus on the less formidable, though still rich in ethnic diversity and quite versatile,

2

recipes of "Old Lithuania." In addition to the obvious Polish and German influences, in the Lithuanian kitchen you will find the influence of the Ukrainians, Ruthenians, Russians and Jews, as well as the stamp of the East. The presence of Tartars and Karaims in Lithuania, along with the movement in eastern trade routes, brought a variety of seasonings (garlic, pepper and other spices) and familiarized the local population with far-away specialties. In time, these exotic dishes became established in the Lithuanian kitchen. In a similar way, the Lithuanians adapted various German dishes, such as potato baba and pyramid cake, into their own way of doing things.

Lithuania has always produced an abundance of foods of every sort. Its forests were famous for their game, mushrooms and berries. Its rivers and lakes teemed with fish and crayfish. Its access to the sea provided salt-water fish as well, while the countryside yielded a profusion of grain, vegetables, milk and honey. The Lithuanians, always noted for their hospitality, also liked to eat well themselves.

What characterizes the Lithuanian kitchen during a time of the confluence of the peasant and manorial kitchen? It is the relatively small quantity of soup the Lithuanians consume, which they replaced with salads and cold dishes of various kinds. Stewing and roasting predominate in their warm dishes. The most commonly used vegetables are: potatoes, beets, turnips, kohlrabi, beans and cabbage. Many mixed salads are prepared from them, served with groats, mushrooms and meat. The tradition of consuming meat is very old here, and Lithuania must be considered the country which introduced to the European kitchen the art of smoking and preserving meat. Its old and tried ways of salting and smoking meat by various methods resulted in the renown of Lithuanian smoked meat products. Another specialty is white cheese, prepared in a variety of ways. The most popular is "Mother's Farmer cheese" (also available in the U.S. in its familiar heart shape), often replacing butter as a spread for bread after being mixed with fat and spices.

A curious item in the Lithuanian kitchen is hemp seed (which is now becoming a novelty item in New York restaurants as well). Lithuanian cookbooks contain many recipes for this plant, (which is a basis for hashish/cannabis), cooked in milk and in other ways. Every Lithuanian vegetable garden once had a spot for a hemp patch. No wonder the Lithuanians seem so content!

Another Lithuanian delicacy which others consider exceedingly strange is cucumbers with honey. Every one should try at least once these cold little cucumbers with aromatic creamy acacia honey.

Two products which play an important role in the Lithuanian kitchen should be mentioned: bread and sour cream. Dark rye bread, baked on a bed of sweet flag, has been prepared since time immemorial, and is used to accompany all three meals of the day. The respect the Lithuanians had for bread is illustrated by the fact that in folklore bread is often a synonym for food. At one time, if a piece of bread happened to fall on the floor, it was mandatory to pick it up and kiss it.

As to sour cream, it is omnipresent in Lithuanian cooking. It is an integral part of many dishes, often replacing other fats. If you place a spoon into Lithuanian sour cream, it will stand bolt upright—no watery consistency will be tolerated!

Drinks such as mead and krupnik, often mentioned in historical novels and poems, are no longer consumed on a regular basis. Kvas, a bread and yeast drink, is still popular, along with beer which, supposedly, "every self-respecting Lithuanian housewife could brew up in a pot." For special occasions, a professional beer maker was engaged, producing a dark-colored but not very potent beer which could be consumed with meals in large quantities.

Today, when abundant larders are a thing of legend, and there is barely time to prepare "powdered soup," let us view some of these recipes as . . . artistic memories, since good cooking is a matter of art, and any clever cook can be its muse. Surely, you will find that some of the dishes described in this book will bring a refreshing change to your daily menu. You must decide for yourself what ingredients you will change to make the dish more dietetic, but remember that too many changes will destroy the authenticity and great taste of these dishes. And keep in mind the old Lithuanian proverb: "As the meat is, so will the soup be."

APPETIZERS
& BREADS

POTATO ZEPPELINS
(Cepeliny)

This is the most popular Lithuanian dish, prepared with various fillings.

7 to 8 medium raw potatoes
4 medium potatoes, boiled
Salt and pepper
2 eggs

1. Peel and grate raw potatoes. Strain through cloth.
2. Add mashed boiled potatoes, salt, pepper and slightly beaten eggs. Combine thoroughly.
3. Pat this mixture into oblong patties about the size of small frankfurter rolls, slightly plumper in the middle.
4. Place a spoonful of filling on each patty and fold potato mixture over it.
5. Drop into boiling water, cooking 20 to 25 minutes.

Some possible fillings for zeppelins:

1. *Meat filling:* ⅓ pound ground beef; ¼ pound ground pork; 1 medium onion, chopped and browned in butter; and salt and pepper to taste. If necessary, a few tablespoons of broth.

2. *Ham or bacon filling:* 1 pound chopped ham or bacon; 1 medium onion, chopped; 1 raw egg; and pepper to taste.

3. *Cottage cheese filling:* 1 pound cottage or farmer's cheese; 1 egg; 1 teaspoon butter; and salt to taste.

4. *Mushroom filling:* 1 pound mushrooms (chopped); ¼ pound bacon; 1 medium chopped onion; salt and pepper to taste; 1 egg; and ½ cup stale roll soaked in milk.

Preparation for mushroom filling: Grind mushrooms together with bacon; add roll after milk has been squeezed out; add egg & seasoning. Mix well.

This variation may be served with sour cream, melted butter or sautéed onion and mushroom sauce.

5. *Sauerkraut filling:* 4 cups sauerkraut; ½ cup bacon; 1 medium onion.
   Preparation of sauerkraut filling: Chop onion, and sauté with chopped bacon; add sauerkraut and cook until mixture becomes soft. Finish cooking without lid, so that excess liquid can evaporate.

All of the above variations may be served with a sautéed onion and bacon mixture and (of course!) sour cream.

Makes about 12 servings in each variation.

LAYERED RIBBON SANDWICHES

Ribbon sandwiches are made from 3 layers of black and white bread with various sandwich toppings.

1. Cut the bread into thin slices and remove the crust. The first layer should be formed from squares of white bread, cut to a desired size. Spread with any kind of appetizer spread, the same thickness as the bread.
2. A layer of black bread comes next, spread with another sandwich filling, followed by a third layer of white bread.
3. Now, the sandwich is pressed together for a few hours, so that the various pieces of bread can fuse.
4. Then, spread the top with anchovy butter or a thin layer of mayonnaise, and sprinkle with finely chopped hard-boiled egg yolk, egg white, smoked ham, and scallions in such a way that each topping forms a stripe.
5. Slice across the design into small 1½ to 2-inch pieces and arrange on a platter.

The fillings for these ribbon sandwiches may be anything you like: smoked meat or fish, cheese, olives, etc.

CHRISTMAS EVE BISCUITS WITH POPPY SEED MILK

Preheat oven to 350 degrees.

1 ounce yeast
1 tablespoon sugar
1 cup warm milk
½ teaspoon salt
1½ cups flour

1. Cream the yeast with the sugar.
2. Add the warm milk and salt. Sift in the flour, stirring thoroughly.
3. Place in a warm spot to rise a little. If necessary, add a bit more flour to roll. Roll with a rolling pin on a floured board.
4. Cut into finger-width strips, then into bits of ½ inch or less.
5. Bake at 350 degrees until edges become brown. Serve with:

Poppy Seed Milk

1½ cups finely ground poppy seeds
2 cups boiling water
10 almonds
Sugar
2 cups milk

1. Cover the ground poppy seeds with boiling water.
2. Blanch, peel, and chop almonds; stir them into the poppy seeds.
3. Add sugar to taste, and when cool, pour in the milk.
4. Pour over the biscuits just before serving.

Makes 4 to 5 servings.

BREADS

POTATO BREAD
(Bulvinis Ragaisis)

1 large raw potato, peeled and finely grated
2 cups scalded milk
1 ounce yeast
8 cups flour, divided
1 egg
3 tablespoons sour cream
1 tablespoon salt
Butter or shortening for greasing pans

1. Add hot milk to grated potato and let stand until lukewarm.
2. Crumble yeast into the mixture (or pour in dry yeast).
3. Add 4 cups of the flour, and mix well with a wooden spoon.
4. Add the egg, sour cream, salt and remaining flour. Beat well. Cover, and let rise for 2 to 3 hours. Beat dough again.
5. Grease 3 bread pans with butter or shortening, fill half-full with batter. Cover with a towel, and let stand until double in size.

Preheat oven to 450 degrees.

6. Bake bread for 15 minutes, before reducing the heat to 350 degrees, and continue baking for 45 minutes more.

Bread will stay moist and fresh for days.

Makes 3 medium loaves.

LITHUANIAN RYE BREAD

1 cup wine vinegar
Boiling water
7 cups dark rye flour
1 to 3 teaspoons salt
1 to 3 teaspoons caraway seeds
¾ cake yeast, divided
½ cup sugar
Enough all-purpose flour to make a stiff dough
Butter or shortening for greasing bread pans
Cracker meal or corn meal for sprinkling over
     bread pans

Dough should be mixed in a wooden pail or bucket (oak, if possible). Season a new pail by rubbing it with salt, finely cut onions, and caraway seeds. If the bucket is used rarely, season it anew before baking. When a freshly seasoned pail is used, decrease the amount of salt and caraway seeds for dough.

1. Dilute the vinegar with an equal amount of boiling water. Stir into the rye flour. Add enough boiled water to make a thin paste.
2. Add salt and caraway seeds. Let mixture cool.
3. Dissolve ½ cake of yeast and sugar in 1 cup lukewarm water. Stir this into the rye mixture while it is still slightly warm. Cover with a cloth.
4. Let stand overnight in a warm, even temperature.
5. In the morning, add the remaining ¼ cake of yeast, which has been dissolved in a little lukewarm water. Stir in enough all-purpose flour to make a stiff dough. Mix vigorously.
6. Let rise for 1 hour.

Preheat oven to 450 degrees.

7. Divide dough in half and place in large bread pans which have been greased with butter or shortening, and sprinkled with cracker meal or corn meal. Let rise again for 15 to 30 minutes.
8. Bake in a 450-degree oven for 20 to 30 minutes, until the tops of the bread are brown, and then reduce the temperature to 350 degrees and continue baking for another 2½ to 3 hours.

Makes 2 large breads.

SOUPS

COLD SUMMER BEET SOUP
(Chlodnik)

1 quart jar prepared borscht with strips of beets
1 medium cucumber, sliced
3 to 4 radishes, sliced
Dill and chives
1 teaspoon grated onion (optional)
Juice of ½ lemon
Dash sugar
2 envelopes (.14 ounces) beef or chicken broth powder
2 to 3 tablespoons sour cream
1 cup buttermilk
3 to 4 hard-boiled eggs for garnish

optional—add thin strips of ham, cold veal roast, or small
    cooked shrimp (better yet, crayfish)

1. Pour part of borscht over sliced cucumber and radishes
   in bowl or serving dish. Season with chopped dill and
   chives to taste.
2. Add lemon, sugar, broth powder, sour cream and buttermilk to liquid remaining in the borscht bottle, and shake
   well with lid on.
3. Add bottle mixture to bowl. Let stand in refrigerator for
   several hours or overnight.
4. Slice or quarter hard-boiled eggs and serve in or along-
   side the soup.

Makes 6 to 8 servings.

CAULIFLOWER SOUP

1 medium cauliflower
6 cups light soup stock (preferably chicken)
1 tablespoon butter
1 tablespoon flour
2 to 3 egg yolks
½ cup heavy or medium sweet cream (or sour cream)
6 fresh mushrooms, cut into strips and sautéed in
    butter (optional)
Salt and pepper, to taste
Croutons for garnish

1. Cook cauliflower in salted boiling water until tender, about 20 to 30 minutes. Reserve 6 to 8 florets.
2. Mash the rest, and combine with hot meat stock.
3. To thicken, add the butter and the flour, stirring to a paste and diluting until smooth. Let simmer another few minutes.
4. Beat egg yolks with cream. Add to soup, a little at a time, stirring constantly to avoid curdling.
5. Season to taste with salt and pepper.
6. Add the reserved florets, mushrooms if desired, and serve with croutons.

Makes 6 to 7 servings.

FRESH CUCUMBER SOUP

4 cups prepared broth or bouillon
2 to 3 medium cucumbers
½ pound smoked ham
1 medium onion, sliced
2 cloves
1 tablespoon flour
1 tablespoon butter
1 cup heavy or medium cream
2 egg yolks
½ cup cooked barley
Salt and pepper
Chopped fresh dill, for garnish

1. Place broth in pot to heat.
2. Peel ⅓ of the cucumbers, slice, and cook in salted water till soft. Drain, rinse with cold water and place into soup tureen.
3. Clean and slice remaining cucumbers, place in a separate pot together with the ham, onion, and cloves.
4. Sauté 1 tablespoon flour in butter. Add to broth and cook.
5. When cucumbers and onions are soft, remove ham and cloves (cut ham into strips to return to soup later); force cucumbers and onions in broth through a sieve or food mill.
6. Beat broth and cream with the egg yolks. Add cooked barley and strips of ham. Add salt and pepper to taste. Heat the soup, but do not boil and add to soup tureen.
7. Sprinkle with fresh dill before serving.

Makes 5 servings.

 **LEMON SOUP**

2 egg yolks
1 tablespoon flour
⅔ cup sour cream
6 cups stock made with veal bones (or 6 cups prepared
  chicken broth)
Grated rind from 1 small to medium lemon
Juice of same lemon

1. Beat raw egg yolks and flour into sour cream until thoroughly smooth.
2. Slowly add hot, strained soup stock, being careful not to let liquid curdle.
3. Add lemon rind.
4. Since tastes differ, add lemon juice a little at a time, or soup may turn out to be too tart.
5. Heat thoroughly on very low heat.

Serve with croutons or hot boiled rice.

Makes 6 to 7 servings.

DILL PICKLE SOUP WITH KIDNEYS

1 pound veal kidneys
3 to 4 medium dill pickles
1 tablespoon butter
6 cups beef stock
1 pound potatoes
1 cup sour cream
Salt and pepper
Pickle juice

1. Boil kidneys in separate pot, changing water several times after it comes to a boil. When kidneys are soft, cut them into thin slices and set aside.
2. Peel the pickles, remove seeds and dice. Braise in the butter and a little broth.
3. Cube potatoes and add to broth, cooking until they are soft. Then add cooked pickles (if pickles are added earlier, potatoes may not soften).
4. Place cut kidneys into soup.
5. Add sour cream with a pinch of salt and stir into soup.
6. After tasting soup, add pickle liquid, a little at a time until desired degree of sourness is achieved. Lemon may be substituted for pickle juice.

Makes 6 to 7 servings.

BEET SOUP WITH VEGETABLES

3 medium red beets
½ head small cabbage (preferably Savoy)
6 cups beef broth
½ pound beef for stew
½ pound smoked pork
1 pound potatoes
4 carrots
2 medium onions
3 tomatoes, cubed
1 cup cooked navy beans
1 cup sour cream
Salt

1. Cook beets separately, peel, and cut small or grate coarsely.
2. Cook shredded cabbage in broth. Add beef and pork, cut up in small pieces, to broth. When cabbage is tender, add the beets.
3. Coarsely chop potatoes, carrots and onion and cook separately in water until tender. Add to broth.
4. Add cubed tomatoes and cooked navy beans to broth.
5. Stir in cream, well beaten with a bit of salt to taste.

If soup is not sour-tasting enough, a little lemon juice may be added. It is hearty enough to serve as a whole meal.

Makes 8 servings.

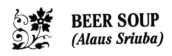

BEER SOUP
(Alaus Sriuba)

1 slice of black bread, toasted
1 stick cinnamon
A few curls orange peel
2 one-pint bottles of beer
2 egg yolks
1 cup sour cream
Salt
1 tablespoon sugar

1. Place toasted bread, cinnamon and orange peel into 2 pints of water (equal to the amount of beer) and cook.
2. After water comes to a boil, strain, add beer and heat in covered pot, just short of bringing to a boil.
3. Beat egg yolks, mix with sour cream, and stir into the soup.
4. Add salt and sugar to taste.

Makes 4 servings.

MUSHROOM AND BARLEY SOUP
(Krupnik)

½ cup barley, to be cooked separately
6 cups beef stock
1½ teaspoons butter
2 to 3 medium potatoes, diced
1 carrot, diced
6 dried mushrooms (soaked in hot water/to be reserved for soup and cut into strips)
½ cup green beans, cut into pieces
Salt and pepper
1 tablespoon chopped parsley

22

1. Cook barley in separate pot, adding a little stock as necessary to separate grains. When done, add butter and stir well. Set aside.
2. Cook potatoes, carrot, mushrooms and beans in stock until tender, adding salt and pepper to taste.
3. Add barley to soup and bring back to a boil. Sprinkle with chopped parsley. Add a little sour cream if desired.

Makes 6 to 7 servings.

 ## BREAD SOUP

6 cups strong beef bouillon
1 tablespoon flour
1 tablespoon butter
6 slices of rye or corn bread
Butter to spread on bread
2 frankfurters or equivalent amount of salami or
    Polish sausage, diced
6 poached eggs
Salt and pepper

1. Thicken the heated bouillon with paste made of dry-browned flour and butter, stirred smooth with a little of the broth. Let simmer.
2. Butter the bread slices and toast in the oven or under the broiler.
3. Dice sausage and add to soup.
4. Pour into individual dishes and top each with a piece of toast on which a poached egg has been placed. Season to taste with salt and pepper.

Makes 6 servings.

CRAYFISH SOUP

20 to 30 live crayfish (about 1 pound fresh shrimp may
    be substituted)
1 bunch fresh dill
Salted water to cover
2 to 3 tablespoons butter
6 cups light soup stock
½ cup sour cream
1 tablespoon flour
1 tablespoon chopped fresh dill

1. Scrub crayfish or shrimp and rinse thoroughly. Add the
   bunch of fresh dill to boiling water and add the crayfish.
   Cook for another 8 to 10 minutes, depending on size.
   Drain, reserving liquid.
2. Shell crayfish, keeping pieces as large as possible, but be
   sure to remove black thread down their backs. Reserve
   shells.
3. Pound shells into a mass, using a mortar and pestle.
   Sauté this mass in a heavy skillet, with butter, for half
   an hour.
4. Combine shells with liquid in which crayfish cooked and
   skim the "coral butter" which floats to the surface to add
   to the soup later.
5. After all "coral butter" has been skimmed, reduce liquid
   to one cup, strain and add to soup stock.
6. Add sour cream blended with the flour and bring to a
   rolling boil once. Add cleaned crayfish meat, the skimmed
   "coral butter" and chopped dill. Season to taste.

Makes 6 to 7 servings.

 **DRIED MUSHROOM SOUP**
(Often served on Christmas Eve)

2 medium onions
1 leek
2 stalks celery
2 carrots
1 parsnip or celery root
7 cups water
½ ounce dried mushrooms
1 tablespoon browned flour (which is heated in a skillet
　　over low flame until it turns light brown before butter
　　is added)
1 tablespoon butter
Salt and pepper

1. Dice or cut into strips all vegetables (except mushrooms,
   which are cut after they become soft). Place all in pot
   with water.
2. Simmer mushrooms and vegetables until thoroughly done
   (about one hour).
3. Remove mushrooms, cut into thin strips and return to
   the pot.
4. Thicken the soup with a paste made of browned flour
   and butter, blend well and season with salt and pepper to
   taste. Flat noodles or macaroni may be added.

Makes 6 to 7 servings.

GREEN SOUP WITH POTATOES

1 small green Savoy cabbage
3 tablespoons butter or lard
1 tablespoon crushed caraway seeds
Salt and pepper
2 medium potatoes, cubed
8 cups beef broth

1. Shred cabbage into fine strips.
2. Melt the butter or lard on medium heat in a large pot. Add the cabbage and fry for a few minutes, stirring well, until wilted.
3. Add the caraway seeds, salt, and freshly ground pepper to taste. Add the potatoes and the broth. Bring to a boil slowly and then reduce the heat.
4. Simmer, partially covered, until done, about 30 minutes.

May be served with croutons made from cubed dark bread fried in butter.

Makes 6 servings.

POTATO SOUP

¼ ounce dried mushrooms
2 slices bacon, finely diced
3 medium onions, finely chopped
2 cloves garlic, crushed
½ medium celeriac, diced
2 medium carrots, diced
1 medium parsnip, diced
8 cups beef broth
6 medium potatoes, cubed
1 teaspoon crushed caraway seeds
1 teaspoon marjoram
Salt and pepper
¼ cup sour cream (optional)

1. Soak the dried mushrooms in warm water for 15 minutes. (Never boil dried mushrooms, since this toughens them.) When softened, chop fine and set aside.
2. Fry the bacon in a large pot over medium heat until well done, but not crisp. Reduce heat and add the onions and garlic. Fry, stirring occasionally, until almost golden.
3. Add the celeriac, carrots and parsnip and sauté for a few minutes. Cover with the broth, bring slowly to a boil, reduce heat and keep on a simmer.
4. Add the reserved mushrooms, potatoes, caraway seeds, marjoram, and salt and pepper to taste.
5. Simmer uncovered for about 20 minutes more, adding sour cream at the end if desired.

Makes 6 servings.

GARLIC SOUP

6 cloves garlic
1 tablespoon salt
8 cups beef broth
1 teaspoon crushed caraway seeds
2 medium potatoes, diced
1 teaspoon marjoram
2 tablespoons butter
½ teaspoon chopped ginger
Salt and pepper
4 slices of dark rye bread
2 tablespoons chopped fresh parsley

1. Mash the garlic with the salt (either use a mortar and pestle or use a garlic press to crush the garlic, and then mix in the salt).
2. Place the garlic and salt in a large pot and add the broth. Slowly bring to a boil, reduce the heat and keep on a simmer.
3. Add the crushed caraway seeds, potatoes, marjoram, butter, and ginger. Simmer, uncovered, until the potatoes are tender, about 15 minutes. Add more salt if needed and pepper to taste.
4. Fry the slices of bread in bacon drippings or butter until golden brown. Place a slice of bread in each soup bowl and ladle the garlic soup over it. Sprinkle with parsley.

Makes 4 servings.

VEGETABLE SOUP WITH DUMPLINGS

4 medium carrots, diced
4 medium potatoes, diced
1 small onion, chopped
½ Savoy cabbage, shredded
1 cup thinly cut string beans
1 cup cauliflower pieces
1 cup fresh peas (or any other fresh vegetables in season)
6 cups chicken broth
1 bay leaf (to be removed before serving)
Salt and pepper
2 tablespoons flour
3 tablespoons butter
2 egg yolks
½ cup heavy cream
Chopped dill for garnish

1. Cook all the vegetables in the broth until they are soft. (Cabbage should first be scalded in boiling water to remove its bitter taste.) Add salt and pepper to taste.
2. Sauté flour in butter and add a little of the broth to it. Then pour it into the soup.
3. Add the dumplings before adding the egg yolks and cream.

Dumplings:

1 tablespoon butter
3 eggs, separated
1 cup flour
Milk as needed

1. Beat the butter, add the egg yolks, and mix well.
2. Add the flour and beaten egg whites (if the dough is too thick, add a little milk).
3. Spoon into the boiling soup.

Beat the egg yolks from the soup recipe with cream and pour into the soup. Do not let the soup come to a full boil, because the egg yolks might scramble.

Garnish with chopped dill before serving.

Makes 6 to 8 servings.

SUMMER SQUASH SOUP WITH EGG NOODLES

3 pounds ripe summer squash, peeled and deseeded
Salt and pepper
2 quarts (8 cups) milk
1½ tablespoons butter

1. Cut the squash into pieces, place in a pot, add water to cover, and salt and pepper to taste. Cook until tender.
2. When the squash is cooked, force it through a strainer, blender, or food mill, and add the milk and butter. Heat but do not boil.

Egg Noodles *(Kukulaiciai)*

2 cups flour
1 egg
Water as needed
Salt

1. Combine flour, egg, and enough water to make a soft dough.
2. Pinch dough into small pieces and cook in a small amount of water. Drain and add noodles to the soup. If the soup is too thick, add a little of the water in which the noodles cooked.
3. Add salt to taste.

GREEN LEAF SOUP

2 pounds soup meat with bones
1 cup raw barley
1 medium turnip, thinly sliced
4 medium potatoes, diced
Small bunch turnip greens (if available), finely chopped
Small bunch beet greens, finely chopped
A few slices bacon, chopped
1 small onion, minced

1. Cook the meat and barley in water. Midway through the cooking (after about 1 hour), add the turnip and potatoes. Continue cooking until the vegetables are tender.
2. Cook the turnip greens and beet greens separately in boiling water. Let them come to a boil twice, and then rinse with cold water.
3. Strain the broth, reserving the cooked meat for another occasion, add the greens and bring to a boil.
4. Sauté bacon and onion and add to the soup. This soup should be thick.

Makes 5 to 6 servings.

 **SAUERKRAUT SOUP**

6 cups beef broth
2 medium tomatoes, diced
2 sour apples, grated
2 medium carrots, grated
2 to 3 dried mushrooms
2 pounds sauerkraut
3 to 4 slices bacon, cubed
4 tablespoons lard (or butter)
1 small onion, grated
2 tablespoons flour

1. Bring the broth to a boil, then add the tomatoes, apples, carrots, and mushrooms. Cook until the vegetables become soft, about 20 minutes.
2. Separately, braise the sauerkraut with the bacon, lard (or butter), and grated onion. Once the sauerkraut is soft, add the mixture into the broth. Add the flour toward the end of the cooking period.

This soup is usually served with boiled or fried potatoes.

Makes 5 to 6 servings.

 **TOMATO SOUP WITH MEAT-FILLED PASTRY**

6 cups beef broth
4 to 5 medium tomatoes
1 tablespoon butter
1 tablespoon potato starch
Chopped parsley for garnish

1. Heat the broth, saving ½ cup for mixing cold with potato starch.
2. Cut the tomatoes into pieces. In a separate pan, cook the tomatoes slightly and force through a strainer, food processor, or food mill. Add the butter to the tomatoes and cook briefly over low heat.
3. Add the tomatoes to the broth. Dissolve the potato starch in the reserved broth and add to the soup. Bring it to a boil and serve with chopped parsley sprinkled over the top of the serving dish.

Pastry:

1 packet yeast
Dash of sugar
1 cup milk
3 cups flour
3 egg yolks
Dash of salt
½ teaspoon grated lemon peel
8 tablespoons butter
1 egg for brushing

1. Mix yeast with a dash of sugar. Add to dough, made using the milk and 1½ cups of the flour. Let the mixture rise in a covered bowl.
2. Beat the egg yolks with a dash of salt.

3. When the dough has risen, beat it well so that there are no lumps, add the egg yolks, the rest of the flour, the lemon peel, and place in a covered bowl to rise once more. Put it in a cool place.
4. When the dough is chilled, roll it out to a thickness of ⅓-inch and dot with some of the butter. Fold the dough into the shape of an envelope and chill.
5. When the dough is chilled, roll it out again, dot with butter, and repeat this process 2 or 3 times.
6. After you roll the dough out for the last time, spread it with the meat filling, roll it up, and put it on a baking sheet to rise. After it has risen, brush the surface with beaten egg and bake in a 350-degree oven for about 20 minutes.

Meat Filling:

1 pound cooked leftover meat (beef, veal, or lamb), ground
1 medium onion, chopped
1 tablespoon butter
2 tablespoons bread crumbs
2 egg yolks
Salt and pepper

1. Using a blender or food processor, grind the meat.
2. Sauté the onion in butter, then add it to the meat, along with the bread crumbs. Grind again.
3. Sauté the mixture, let it cool, add the egg yolks and salt and pepper to taste. Blend well, and spread over the prepared dough.

Before serving, cut into 1-inch slices and arrange on a platter so that the edge of one slice overlaps the previous slice.

Soup makes 5 to 6 servings.

FISH SOUP WITH DUMPLINGS AND POTATO BALLS

3 pounds fish (any firm-fleshed fish you like)
6 cups light broth (or your own chicken or fish soup stock)
1 tablespoon flour
2 tablespoons butter
2 cups sour cream
Chopped parsley for garnish

1. Boil the fish in broth for about 30 minutes. Strain, discarding the fish.
2. Sauté the flour in butter and add to the broth.
3. Add the dumplings and potatoes (recipes follow) to the soup and stir in the sour cream.

Sprinkle with chopped parsley before serving.

Dumplings:

½ pound boned fish
1 small onion, grated
1 tablespoon butter
3 tablespoons bread crumbs
Dash of nutmeg
Salt and pepper
1 tablespoon sour cream
1 egg
Flour for rolling

1. Grind the fish in a blender or food processor.
2. Sauté the onion in the butter.
3. Add the onion, bread crumbs, nutmeg, and salt and pepper to taste. Add the sour cream and egg to the fish and blend well.
4. Shape the mixture into small dumplings.
5. Roll each dumpling in flour and cook it in the fish broth for about 15 minutes.

Potato Balls:

Using as large potatoes as you can find, cut round shapes from them. (A metal melon baller usually works well for this.) Boil these balls in salted water separately, and add to the soup when they are tender.

Makes 7 to 8 servings

 ## CHERRY SOUP

2 pounds fresh cherries, pitted
Juice of ½ lemon
Sugar
Cinnamon
1 tablespoon potato starch
1 cup sour cream

1. Cover cherries with boiling water, add lemon juice (to retain color), sugar, and cinnamon. Simmer for 10 to 15 minutes.
2. Add the potato starch, dissolved in a little cold water, and bring to a boil. Chill.
3. Stir in sour cream before serving.

Home-made egg dumplings (leistinukai) may be cooked separately and added to this soup, or it may be served with croutons.

Dumplings *(Leistinukai)*:

1 cup flour
1 tablespoon butter
1 egg
Pinch of salt
Enough water to make a loose dough

Mix all of the above ingredients and drop into boiling water by the teaspoonful. Cool before adding to the soup.

Makes 5 to 6 servings.

 ## BLUEBERRY SOUP WITH DUMPLINGS

3 cups blueberries
Peel of 1 lemon, in strips
Cinnamon
6 cups water
1 cup sugar
1 cup sour cream

1. Pick over the blueberries, add lemon peel and cinnamon. Add the water and cook for about 20 minutes.
2. When berries are done, put them through a blender or strainer, first removing the lemon peel.
3. Add the sugar and sour cream and then heat, but do not bring to a boil.

Prepare accompanying dumplings as in the recipe for cherry soup above.

Makes 6 to 7 servings.

COLD APPLE SOUP WITH BREAD CRUMB DUMPLINGS

5 medium apples, cut into sections
Peel of 1 orange
Cinnamon
3 cups water
1 cup apple juice
1 cup sugar

1. Place the apples in a pot, and add the orange peel and cinnamon. Cover with water and cook until tender.
2. After removing the orange peel, process in blender or put through strainer. Add the apple juice and sugar and heat but do not boil. Chill.

Bread Crumb Dumplings *(Leistiniai)*:

2 tablespoons sugar
2 eggs
Enough bread crumbs to make a thick dough
2 medium apples, peeled and grated

1. Add the sugar, eggs, and enough bread crumbs to make a thick dough to the apples. Beat well.
2. Spoon the dough, using a teaspoon, into boiling water.
3. When the dumplings rise to the surface, remove them from the water. Cool and add to the soup. Chill before serving.

Makes 5 to 6 servings.

LITHUANIAN BORSCHT

2 pounds soup meat (beef chuck)
3 medium marrow bones
3½ quarts cold water
1 medium Savoy cabbage, finely shredded
2 medium onions, chopped
4 to 5 medium tomatoes, sliced
1 small can tomato purée
3 bay leaves
½ cup brown sugar
2 teaspoons seasoned salt
½ teaspoon sour salt (citric acid)
Salt and pepper
½ teaspoon powdered yeast
½ cup chopped parsley
¼ cup fresh chopped dill
Juice of 1 lemon

1. Place the meat and bones into the water in a large pot. When the water boils, skim off the foam, then cover and simmer for one hour.
2. Add the cabbage, onions, tomatoes, purée, bay leaves, brown sugar, seasoned salt, sour salt, salt (regular) and pepper, powdered yeast, parsley, and dill.
3. Cook over a slow flame until the meat is tender, adding the lemon juice near the end of the cooking period (of about 2½ hours).

May be served with a dollop of sour cream, if desired.

Makes 5 to 6 servings.

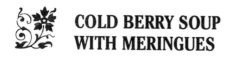

COLD BERRY SOUP WITH MERINGUES

7 cups berries (raspberries, currants, or strawberries)
1½ cups sugar
4 cups sour cream
A few handfuls of whole berries
½ cup white wine (optional)
Meringues (recipe follows)

1. Put the berries through a blender or food processor. Add the sugar and the sour cream.
2. Chill overnight and add a handful of whole berries to each plate before serving.

Meringues:

3 egg whites
1 teaspoon vanilla
¼ teaspoon cream of tartar
Dash of salt
1 cup sugar

Preheat oven to 225 degrees.

1. Have the egg whites at room temperature. Add the vanilla, cream of tartar, and salt.
2. Beat until frothy. Gradually add the sugar, a small amount at a time, beating until very stiff peaks form and sugar is dissolved. The mixture should be shiny.
3. Cover a cookie sheet with plain ungreased paper (can be part of brown paper bag or typing paper).
4. Using a teaspoon, drop meringues onto the cookie sheet, about 1 inch apart.
5. Bake in a very slow oven (225 degrees) for about 45 minutes. Then shut off the oven and keep the meringues

in for another 45 minutes or so until they are thoroughly dry.

Makes 10 to 12 servings of the soup, and 20 to 30 small meringues, depending on exact size desired.

VEGETABLES
& SALADS

BRAISED BEETS
(Good served with lamb roast)

3 pounds red beets
1 medium onion, grated finely
2 tablespoons butter
2 tablespoons flour
Salt
Pepper
Sugar
Lemon juice
½ cup sour cream

1. Cook unpeeled beets or bake in oven until soft.
2. Peel and grate them coarsely.
3. Grate onion and sauté in butter, adding flour.
4. Add grated beets, salt, pepper, sugar, lemon juice to taste. Braise, stirring occasionally for 5 minutes.
5. Add sour cream just before serving.

Makes 8 to 10 servings.

LETTUCE WITH SOUR CREAM

2 small heads soft lettuce (such as bib, Boston, or similar)
3 hard-boiled eggs
1 teaspoon sugar
Juice of 1 lemon
1 cup sour cream
Salt

1. Wash and dry lettuce thoroughly and set aside in a cool place.
2. Separate hard-boiled egg yolks and egg whites. Grate the yolks and mix with the sugar. Cut the egg whites into

small chunks to garnish the salad before serving.

3. Mix the lemon juice with the sour cream and add to the egg yolks. Add salt to taste.
4. Pour the mixture over the lettuce, garnish with the egg whites, and serve at once.

Makes 5 to 6 servings.

 ## FRIED CARROTS

2 bunches carrots, blanched (very young carrots may be
    used whole, unpeeled; older ones should be scraped
    and cut in halves or quarters)
1 to 2 tablespoons butter
Salt and pepper
¼ cup bouillon, water or orange juice
Sugar
Lemon juice

1. Blanch, then simmer tightly covered carrots with butter, salt and pepper to taste, and bouillon.
2. When steamed through, add sugar for a sweet taste and lemon for balance, and continue cooking uncovered, stirring constantly, until sauce thickens and carrots begin to brown.

Makes 5 to 6 servings.

STUFFED CUCUMBERS

6 to 8 cucumbers (medium sized, all of even size)
Thin bacon strips to cover
1 cup strong bouillon
½ teaspoon Maggi or similar extract
3 ounces Madeira or sherry

For stuffing:

½ medium onion, grated
1½ teaspoons butter
½ pound ground veal, raw or leftover roast or
    ½ pound raw boned fish
1 stale white roll, moistened in milk and mashed
    (or bread crumbs)
Salt and pepper
1 egg, lightly beaten

1. Peel cucumbers and cut in half lengthwise and scoop out seeds. Blanch in boiling salted water.
2. To make stuffing, brown onion lightly in butter. Combine all of the remaining stuffing ingredients, mix thoroughly and fill cucumber halves.
3. Arrange tightly in a deep sauce pan, cover with bacon strips and add bouillon. Simmer, tightly covered, until transparent and completely done, about 30 minutes.
4. Brown flour in a dry skillet, taking care not to burn. Dilute with a little of the sauce, add Maggi extract and Madeira, and pour over cucumbers. Allow to boil up.

Makes 4 to 5 servings

PURÉE OF BEETS AND APPLES

5 to 6 medium beets
2 sour apples
1 tablespoon bacon fat
Salt and pepper
Lemon juice
Sugar
2 to 3 tablespoons sour cream
1½ teaspoons flour

1. Peel beets and apples and grate coarsely, reserving all the juices.
2. Melt bacon fat and add grated beets and apples, together with all their juices.
3. Season with salt and pepper, adding lemon juice and sugar to taste.
4. Simmer, covered, for half an hour, then uncover and reduce liquid, adding sour cream combined with the flour. Let boil up and simmer for a few more minutes.

Excellent with roasts.

Makes 6 servings.

POTATO, APPLE AND CAPER SALAD

6 medium unpeeled potatoes, cooked in salted water
2 medium sour apples (such as Granny Smith)
1 heaping tablespoon capers
¼ cup olive oil
¼ cup dry white wine
Lemon juice
Salt and pepper

1. Peel potatoes and allow to cool.
2. Core and peel the apples.
3. Slice potatoes and apples very thin, mix with capers, olive oil, wine and lemon juice to taste. Season with salt and pepper sparingly, since capers are salty in themselves.
4. Refrigerate one hour before serving.

Makes 6 servings.

FRIED TOMATOES

1 egg
½ cup milk
⅔ cup flour
3 large, unripe tomatoes
3 to 4 tablespoons butter or vegetable oil for frying
2 tablespoons fresh chopped parsley
Wedges of lemon for garnish

1. To make batter, break the egg into a bowl and mix in the milk. Slowly, add the flour, mixing well, until you have a fairly thick batter.

Preheat oven to warm.

2. Cut the tomatoes into thick slices.
3. Heat butter in a large frying pan over medium heat. When the pan is heated, dip a tomato slice in the batter, then place it in the frying pan. Continue doing this until the pan is fairly full, but not crowded. Make several batches if necessary.
4. Fry the tomatoes until lightly golden on both sides, about 7 to 8 minutes altogether. Remove and keep warm in the oven. Repeat this procedure until all the tomatoes are fried. Drain tomatoes on paper towels to remove excess oil.

Serve sprinkled with parsley and lemon wedges.

Makes 4 servings.

SOUR POTATOES

8 large potatoes
2 tablespoons butter
2 tablespoons flour
1 cup milk
½ cup white vinegar
½ cup sour cream
2 tablespoons fresh chopped dill
Salt and pepper

1. Boil the whole, unpeeled potatoes in a large pot filled with salted water until tender, about 30 minutes.
2. Meanwhile, prepare the sauce. Melt the butter in a frying pan on medium heat. Stir in the flour and cook for 2 minutes.
3. Pour in the milk while stirring constantly. Reduce the heat and let boil for 1 to 2 minutes.
4. Mix in the vinegar, sour cream, and dill. Season to taste with salt and pepper.
5. Peel the potatoes and slice them thickly. Coat with the sauce and serve.

Makes 4 to 6 servings.

 ## POTATO-BUCKWHEAT GROAT "PRAZUCHA"

2 cups cooked buckwheat groats (recipe follows)
2 cups grated raw potatoes (liquid not squeezed out)
Salt
1 small onion, chopped finely
1 tablespoon butter
Crumbled bacon bits, melted butter or sour cream for garnish

Recipe for buckwheat groats:

1 cup whole buckwheat groats
1 egg
2 cups boiling water
Salt

1. Mix groats with raw egg. Place on dry, pre-heated frying pan and heat until each grain is separate.
2. Add 2 cups boiling water. Cover and cook on medium heat for about 20 minutes, or until all liquid is absorbed.
3. At the end of cooking, add salt to taste. If you prefer, you may skip the salt and add broth instead of water.

Recipe for "prazucha":

1. Grate raw potatoes, leaving potato liquid.
2. Add to pan containing cooked buckwheat groats. Add salt if necessary.
3. Cook together for about 10 minutes.
4. While groats and potatoes are cooking, sauté onion in butter until almost golden. Add to groat-potato mixture at the end of cooking period and mix well.

May be served with crumbled bacon bits, melted butter or sour cream as an accompaniment to a meat dish or as a light lunch by itself.

Makes 5 to 6 servings.

RAW VEGETABLE SALAD

2 medium tart apples, grated
2 carrots, grated
3 medium boiled potatoes, cubed
2 medium cucumbers, cubed
1 cup grated rutabaga
1 tablespoon caraway seeds
Salt
2 tablespoons horseradish
½ cup sour cream

1. Grate peeled apples and carrots.
2. Add cubed potatoes, cucumbers and grated rutabaga. Mix well.
3. Add caraway seeds and salt to taste.
4. Combine sour cream with horseradish and add to vegetable mixture.

This salad goes well with baked ham or boiled white sausage.

Makes 4 to 6 servings.

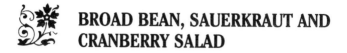

BROAD BEAN, SAUERKRAUT AND CRANBERRY SALAD

2 cups broad beans (if not available, fava or
    dried lima beans)
2 cups sauerkraut
1 teaspoon sugar
2 medium onions, sliced
½ cup olive oil
½ cup fresh cranberries
1 teaspoon caraway seeds
Salt and pepper

1. Soak broad beans overnight. Boil in salted water
   according to directions. When cooked, remove skins.
2. Add sauerkraut (if it seems too salty, drain a bit of its
   liquid and add a little sugar to tame it).
3. Sauté onion in the oil until almost golden. Add onions,
   together with the hot oil, to the bean and sauerkraut
   mixture.
4. Add the washed and dried cranberries, caraway seeds,
   and salt and pepper to taste.

Fresh cabbage may also be used in this salad instead of the
sauerkraut. It should be shredded, sprinkled liberally with
lemon juice, placed between two plates, and shaken until it
releases its juices.

Makes 4 to 6 servings.

VEGETABLE SALAD

5 medium potatoes, cooked
4 medium carrots, cooked
5 hard-boiled eggs, peeled and cooled
½ cup any left-over meat (pork, beef, veal, sausage),
    (optional)
1 medium onion (preferably red), chopped
2 medium sour pickles, cubed
½ cup mayonnaise
¼ cup sour cream
Salt and pepper
1 cup cooked peas
1 tablespoon chopped chives or scallions

1. Cube potatoes, three of the carrots (reserving one for garnish), eggs, and meat (if used). Add chopped onion and cubed pickle.
2. Add the mayonnaise and sour cream and stir to mix. Add salt and pepper to taste.
3. Add peas and mix in gently.
4. Decorate top of the salad with one carrot (cut into a fan shape) and sprinkle with chives.

Makes 6 to 7 servings.

SAVOY CABBAGE WITH CHESTNUTS

1 medium head of Savoy cabbage
½ teaspoon salt
2 cups boiling water
½ pound chestnuts, cooked and peeled (or canned
    whole chestnuts)
2 tablespoons butter
2 tablespoons flour

1. Cut the cabbage into small sections. Cook in the salted boiling water until tender (about 20 to 25 minutes).
2. Drain, reserving the cooking liquid.
3. Slice the chestnuts and add to the cabbage.
4. Melt the butter, add the flour, then stir in the liquid reserved from the cabbage. Stir until the mixture comes to a boil and becomes a smooth sauce.
5. Combine with the cabbage and chestnuts. Cook for 10 minutes longer.

Makes 6 servings.

POTATO BAKE WITH COTTAGE CHEESE

5 medium potatoes, pared and diced
1 teaspoon salt
1 pound cottage cheese
1 tablespoon butter
½ cup heavy cream

Preheat oven to 375 degrees.

1. Arrange half of the potatoes in a greased baking dish. Sprinkle with half of the salt.
2. Press the cheese through a strainer or food mill, letting half of it fall over the first layer of potatoes.
3. Add half of the butter and half of the cream. Repeat with another layer of potatoes, salt, cheese, butter and cream.
4. Bake in 375-degree oven for about 1 hour.

Makes 6 servings.

LAYERED POTATOES WITH HAM

6 medium cooked potatoes, pared and sliced
3 hard-boiled eggs
1 teaspoon salt
1 cup sour cream
½ cup chopped boiled ham
½ cup bread crumbs
2 tablespoons melted butter
½ cup heavy cream

1. Cook the potatoes until almost tender. Pare and slice. Arrange one third of the slices on a greased baking dish.

Preheat oven to 450 degrees.

2. Slice eggs and place over potatoes. Sprinkle with salt.
3. Cover with half of the sour cream.
4. Make another layer of potato slices, then one of ham, covered with the rest of the cream and a final layer of potatoes.
5. Top with the bread crumbs mixed with the melted butter. Add the heavy cream for moistness.
6. Bake in 450-degree oven for about 30 minutes, or until the bread crumbs turn brown.

Makes 4 to 5 servings.

CARROT AND APPLE SALAD

3 medium carrots, peeled
2 sour apples, peeled
Salt
2 tablespoons sour cream
Sugar
Lemon juice

1. Grate carrots and apples coarsely.
2. Add salt and sour cream and mix.
3. If mixture is bland when tasted after mixing, a bit of sugar and lemon juice may be added.

Makes 3 to 4 servings.

 ## RED BEET SALAD

8 medium red beets, peeled and sliced
1 medium onion, minced
Dressing to taste, composed of:
Salt, pepper, lemon juice, and oil

1. Cook beets or bake in the oven.
2. Add minced onion and pour dressing over both.
3. Let stand 2 to 3 hours before serving to let dressing soak into the beets.

Makes 5 to 6 servings.

 # RED BEET SALAD WITH HORSERADISH

Prepare marinade for beet salad as follows:

2 cups water
1 cup wine vinegar
1 bay leaf
6 peppercorns
1 teaspoon sugar
Salt

Boil marinade for about 30 minutes. Cool before adding to the salad.

Beet Salad:

4 medium beets, boiled and grated
1 medium fresh horseradish, grated (or equivalent in prepared horseradish)

1. Peel boiled beets and grate coarsely.
2. Place in a glass dish in layers, alternating with grated horseradish.
3. Pour in cooled marinate. Cover dish tightly and let stand in a cool place for 24 to 48 hours.
4. Remove marinade before serving.

This salad is good served with dark meat dishes and herring.

Makes 3 to 4 servings.

TOMATOES STUFFED WITH SALAD

6 medium firm tomatoes (reserve pulp)
Salt and pepper
1 small bunch radishes, cut in small pieces
1 small head bib lettuce, cut in small pieces
3 scallions, cut in small pieces
2 tablespoons sour cream
2 tablespoons chopped dill

1. Cut off tops of firm tomatoes, scooping out pulp and seeds. Sprinkle with salt and pepper to taste.
2. Save some of the tomato pulp to mix with the radishes, lettuce, and scallions.
3. Add sour cream to the mixed vegetables, along with additional salt and pepper to taste.
4. Stuff the tomatoes with the mixture and sprinkle with chopped dill.

Makes 6 servings as a side dish.

EGGS STUFFED WITH MUSHROOMS

3 hard-boiled eggs
1 small onion, chopped fine
2 tablespoons olive oil
1 cup fresh chopped mushrooms
Salt and pepper
6 mushroom caps for garnish
2 tablespoons butter, divided
3 small cucumbers (of the Kirby type), sliced
½ cup sour cream
Lemon juice
Chopped dill

1. Halve hard-boiled eggs lengthwise, and remove yolks. Set yolks aside.
2. Sauté onion in oil, adding the chopped mushrooms after the onion has browned a little.
3. Cool this mixture, and then add salt and pepper to taste.
4. Stuff the egg halves with the mixture.
5. Sauté the mushroom caps in 1 tablespoon of the butter and place them on top of each egg as garnish.
6. Place sliced cucumbers in one row in the middle of a serving platter. Mix sour cream with lemon juice and additional salt and pepper to taste, and pour this sauce over the cucumbers. Sprinkle with chopped dill.
7. Arrange stuffed egg halves around the cucumbers.
8. Cream the remaining butter with the egg yolks, shape into little balls and place on cucumber slices.

Makes 3 to 4 servings.

POTATO PUDDING I
(Kugelis)

2 cups scalded milk
4 pounds raw potatoes, peeled and grated
1 medium onion, chopped
¼ pound bacon, chopped
Salt and pepper
4 eggs, separated

Preheat oven to 450 degrees.

1. Pour scalded milk over the potatoes. Sauté onion with the chopped bacon and the egg yolk. Add salt and pepper to taste. Mix all together thoroughly.
2. Fold in beaten egg whites. Pour mixture into a greased roasting pan. Bake at 450 degrees for 20 minutes, and then lower the heat to 350 degrees for another 20 minutes, or until golden in color.
3. Slice into oblong pieces.

May be served with additional sautéed chopped bacon, sour cream, or cranberry sauce.

Makes 8 to 10 servings.

POTATO PUDDING II
(Kugelis)

3 pounds raw potatoes (about 9 medium)
1 pound boiled potatoes (about 3 medium)
1 egg
½ cup milk
1 tablespoon farina
1 teaspoon baking powder
4 tablespoons butter
Salt and pepper

Preheat oven to 450 degrees.

1. Grate the raw and boiled potatoes together.
2. Add the egg, milk, farina, baking powder, butter, and salt and pepper to taste. Mix well.
3. Pour into a greased roasting pan and bake at 450 degrees for 20 minutes, then reduce heat to 350 degrees and continue baking for another 20 minutes, or until top turns golden.
4. Serve in the dish it was baked in, along with sour cream or cranberry sauce.

Makes 8 to 10 servings.

 **CABBAGE CAKE**

1 packet dry yeast
1 teaspoon sugar
1 cup warm milk
3½ cups flour
3 egg yolks
Salt
4 tablespoons melted butter
1 beaten egg for brushing

1. Mix yeast with sugar, add warm milk and ⅓ of the flour. Beat well. Put in a warm place to rise.
2. When it rises, beat well again, and gradually add egg yolks beaten with salt and the remaining flour. Knead well.
3. Add melted butter toward end of kneading and knead again. Put in a warm place to rise once more.
4. When it rises, divide into two parts. Roll out to the thickness of one finger. Place one layer on a greased baking sheet, spread with cabbage filling (recipe follows), sprinkle with chopped, hard-boiled eggs and finely chopped dried mushrooms which have been soaked to soften separately.

Preheat oven to 375 degrees.

5. Put another layer of dough on top and leave to rise once again. When it rises, brush with beaten egg, prick the top with a fork so it will lie flat, and bake at 375 degrees for 40 to 50 minutes.

Makes 10 to 12 servings.

Cabbage Filling:

1 medium onion, chopped
4 tablespoons butter
3 pounds sauerkraut, drained of juices
2 bay leaves
Salt and pepper
4 dried mushrooms, soaked to soften and finely chopped
3 hard-boiled eggs, chopped

1. Sauté onion in butter; mix with sauerkraut, bay leaves and salt and pepper to taste.
2. Spread this mixture over the lower layer of dough and sprinkle with chopped mushrooms and hard-boiled eggs.
3. Cover with the second sheet of dough and bake as described above.

Makes 10 to 12 servings.

 ## RED CABBAGE SALAD

1 medium head of red cabbage
2 tablespoons wine vinegar or lemon juice
3 tablespoons olive oil
Salt
Sugar

1. Remove the tough outer leaves from the cabbage and cut the cabbage finely. (For a more tender salad, the cabbage may be scalded before cutting.)
2. Pour a mixture of vinegar (or lemon juice) and olive oil over the cabbage and let stand for 2 to 3 hours to soften.
3. Add salt and sugar to taste.

A possible variation would be to use ½ red and ½ green cabbage for this salad for a nice color effect.

Makes 5 to 6 servings.

KOHLRABI STUFFED WITH MEAT

6 medium kohlrabis
1 pound ground beef or leftover meat (beef, veal, or lamb)
1 medium onion, finely chopped
Salt and pepper
3 tablespoons butter, divided
2 eggs
1½ cups broth
1 cup sour cream

1. Place the kohlrabis into boiling water and parboil for 20 to 30 minutes. Cool until they are easy to handle.

Preheat oven to 350 degrees.

2. Cut off the tops. Using a serrated teaspoon, scrape out the inside, leaving thin walls (which are still strong enough to hold the stuffing), which is prepared as follows:

Stuffing:

3. Grind the meat, add the onion, salt and pepper to taste, kohlrabi pieces sautéed in 1½ tablespoons butter, and the eggs. Mix all well and stuff the kohlrabi.
4. Put the top of the kohlrabi back on, place the kohlrabis into a greased roasting pan, adding the broth and the remaining butter.
5. Bake in a 350-degree oven for about 40 minutes, basting frequently. When almost done, stir in the sour cream.

Serve with the pan gravy.

Makes 6 servings.

TOMATOES STUFFED WITH EGGS

6 medium tomatoes
3 hard-boiled eggs
1 raw egg
1 tablespoon bread crumbs
1 tablespoon chopped parsley
Salt and pepper
4 tablespoons butter

Preheat oven to 350 degrees.

1. Cut off the tops of the tomatoes and, using a serrated spoon, remove most of the pulp.
2. Place the tomatoes in a baking dish and fill with the stuffing, consisting of the hard-boiled eggs, the raw egg, the bread crumbs, parsley and salt and pepper to taste.
3. Cover the tomatoes with their tops and place in a greased baking pan, dotting the tops with butter.
4. Bake at 350 degrees for about 20 minutes, occasionally basting with their pan liquid.

Makes 6 servings.

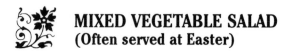 **MIXED VEGETABLE SALAD**
(Often served at Easter)

4 medium potatoes, cooked and cubed
4 medium beets, cooked and cubed
4 medium carrots, cooked and cubed
1 cup cooked white kidney beans
1 cup cooked peas
1 cup cubed dill pickles
2 tart apples, peeled and cubed
1 medium red onion, chopped fine
4 tablespoons olive oil
4 tablespoons wine vinegar
3 hard-boiled eggs, chopped
1 cup sour cream
½ cup mayonnaise
3 tablespoons fresh chopped dill
Salt and pepper
1 hard-boiled egg for garnish
A few decorated radishes for garnish

** You may substitute other vegetables you like better than
the ones listed here.**

1. Cook each vegetable separately. Cool before mixing all
   the vegetables and apples together.
2. Cover with a marinade of oil and vinegar and let stand for
   a couple of hours. Pour off liquid.
3. Place the vegetables and apples into a large salad bowl,
   adding the hard-boiled eggs, sour cream, and mayonnaise. Add dill and salt and pepper to taste.
4. Garnish with hard-boiled egg sections and radishes.

Makes 12 to 15 servings.

MUSHROOMS AND SAUERKRAUT
(Grybai su Kopustais)

½ cup dried mushrooms, soaked in hot water and
    chopped fine
2 cups sauerkraut, rinsed and drained
Salt and pepper
1 tablespoon flour
1 tablespoon butter

1. Mix together mushrooms and sauerkraut, along with salt
   and pepper to taste. Simmer for about 30 minutes.
2. At the end of this time, stir in the flour and butter. Continue simmering, stirring occasionally, until the sauerkraut
   is soft.

Makes 3 to 4 servings.

PEARS SERVED AS A VEGETABLE

6 to 7 firm medium pears, peeled and quartered
2 tablespoons butter
2 tablespoons bread crumbs

1. Cook the pears (preferably a variety which is not too
   sweet) over steam until they are soft when pricked with
   a fork.
2. Melt the butter and bread crumbs and cook until golden.
3. Remove the pears carefully and place on a platter along
   with a variety of vegetables being served.
4. Pour over bread crumb mixture.

Makes 6 to 7 servings.

 **BAKED POTATO DUMPLINGS**
(Bandukes)

5 medium potatoes, boiled and unpeeled
1½ cups flour, plus a little for flouring
2 teaspoons salt
1 small onion, diced fine
1 stick butter
1 cup sweet cream

Preheat oven to 400 degrees.

1. Mash potatoes.
2. Add the flour and salt. Roll into strips on a floured board and cut diagonally into small diamond shapes.
3. Bake in a 400-degree oven for about 30 minutes.

While they are baking, prepare the sauce:

4. Fry the diced onion in butter. When the onion is tender, add the cream. Pour over the baked dumplings and serve immediately.

Makes 4 to 5 servings.

POTATO AND HORSERADISH BAKE

6 to 7 medium potatoes, peeled
¾ cup horseradish (either fresh grated or prepared)
2 cups heavy cream
Salt and pepper

Preheat oven to 400 degrees.

1. Make thin slices of the potatoes by hand or with a mandolin. Spread half of the potatoes on the bottom of an iron pan which can go into the oven.
2. Cover with a layer of horseradish, and then again with a layer of potatoes.
3. Pour over the cream, and place into the oven uncovered for 15 minutes.
4. Cover the pan with foil and continue baking for another 40 minutes. Add salt and pepper to taste.

Serve in the pan in which it cooked.

Makes 5 to 6 servings.

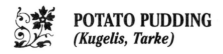

POTATO PUDDING
(Kugelis, Tarke)

5 slices bacon
10 large potatoes, peeled and grated
1 medium onion, peeled and grated
½ cup hot milk
3 eggs
Salt and pepper
Butter for greasing
1 cup sour cream

Preheat oven to 400 degrees.

1. Cut the bacon into narrow strips, fry until crisp, and pour fat and bacon over the potatoes and onion.
2. Add the hot milk and the eggs, one at a time, beating well after each addition. Add salt and pepper to taste.
3. Pour into a baking pan greased with butter and bake at 400 degrees for 15 minutes. Reduce the heat to 375 degrees, and continue baking for another 45 minutes.
4. Cut into squares. Serve hot with sour cream.

Makes 7 to 9 servings.

MUSHROOM PUDDING

1 medium onion, finely chopped
4 tablespoons butter, divided
1 pound fresh mushrooms (white, or even better, shitake
    or portobello), finely chopped
2 to 3 tablespoons water
8 tablespoons bread crumbs, divided
4 eggs, divided
½ cup sour cream
Salt and pepper
Fresh dill for sprinkling

1. Brown onion in 2 tablespoons of the butter and add the mushrooms after the onion has browned a little. Add 2 to 3 tablespoons of water, and cook slowly under cover.

Preheat oven to 350 degrees.

2. When mushrooms are soft, let them cool slightly.
3. Grease a pudding form with the remaining butter and sprinkle it with 2 tablespoons of the bread crumbs.
4. Beat the egg yolks until smooth and light. Add the mushrooms to the egg yolks, alternating with the sour cream.
5. Add the remaining bread crumbs and the beaten egg whites, folding in salt and pepper to taste.
6. Place the pudding form in a pan of warm water (2 to 3 inches) and bake for about 45 minutes at 350 degrees.

Serve with melted butter mixed with bread crumbs poured over the pudding and a sprinkling of fresh dill.

Makes 3 to 4 servings.

ASPICS,
GARNISHES
& SAUCES

ASPICS

 ## PIGS' KNUCKLES JELLY

4 fresh pigs' knuckles (about 2 pounds)
1 large onion
4 carrots
2 celery stalks
5 peppercorns
Sprig of parsley
2 bay leaves
1 cup white wine
Juice of ½ lemon
2 egg whites (beaten), along with their shells
Lemon wedges for garnish
Horseradish for garnish

1. Place knuckles and whole onion, carrots, and celery stalk with peppercorns, parsley, and bay leaves into pot with cold water to cover.
2. Simmer until meat separates easily from the bones (1½ to 2 hours).
3. Remove vegetables from broth (saving carrots for later decoration of bottom of mold). Cool meat and remove from the bones.
4. Strain broth and reheat, adding wine and lemon juice. When liquid comes to a full boil, add egg whites (beaten lightly with a little water), and then their shells. (This will absorb any impurities floating in the liquid and create a clear broth.) Strain.
5. Arrange carrot slices (which could be cut to a star (or other) shape with small cutter), and meat pieces at the bottom of the mold. Pour broth into mold and place in cool place to jell.

Serve with wedges of lemon and horseradish on the side.

Makes 4 to 5 servings.

GARNISHES

 MEAT POCKETS FOR BORSCHT
(Little Ears)

Dough:

2 cups flour
1 large or 2 small eggs
A few teaspoons of water as needed

Filling:

2 cups leftover beef or veal with all fat removed
1 hard roll, moistened in milk
Salt and pepper
2 teaspoons fresh chopped herbs (optional)
1 small onion, chopped and browned in butter
1 tablespoon butter

1. Make dough, mixing flour, eggs and water together well. Work until firm. Roll into a very thin sheet. Cut into 3-inch squares. Keep covered with towel to avoid drying.
2. Grind meat and roll in food processor or blender. Season with salt and pepper to taste and herbs if desired.
3. Mix well and cook with the browned onion for 3 to 5 minutes.
4. Place a teaspoon of this mixture on each dough square. Fold into a triangle and press sides firmly together.
5. Cook in a large amount of boiling salted water for 20 to 30 minutes. The pockets are done when they float to the surface.

Makes 8 to 10 servings to accompany borscht or mushroom soup.

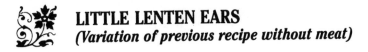

LITTLE LENTEN EARS
(Variation of previous recipe without meat)

Make dough as for Meat Pockets. Fill as follows:

Filling:

½ pound fresh mushrooms, chopped fine
1 small onion, chopped fine
1 tablespoon butter
2 tablespoons bread crumbs
Salt and pepper

Sauté all ingredients together until mushrooms are done and onions are golden brown, taking care not to burn (about 15 minutes).

Proceed as for meat pockets.

Makes 8 to 10 servings.

SAUCES

 ## SWEET RAISIN SAUCE FOR TONGUE

1 tablespoon butter
1 tablespoon flour
1¼ cups bouillon
½ cup white wine
3 tablespoons sugar (or honey)
¼ cup chopped almonds
½ cup raisins
2 teaspoons wine vinegar
½ lemon, sliced

1. Melt the butter with flour and add the bouillon and wine, stirring to smooth.
2. Caramelize the sugar or honey in a pan until it turns light brown and add to the sauce.
3. Add the almonds, raisins, additional sugar, and vinegar and bring to a rapid boil. Just before serving, add the sliced lemon and bring to a boil again.

Makes 2 to 3 cups of sauce.

ONION SAUCE WITH CARAWAY

3 large onions, sliced
3 cups bouillon
Salt and pepper
2 tablespoons butter
2 tablespoons flour
1 tablespoon caraway seeds

1. Cook the onions in bouillon until they are soft. Add salt and pepper to taste.
2. Melt the butter in a pan, adding the flour and the onions with their liquid. Stir well. Add the caraway seeds and continue cooking for 10 minutes more.

Makes 3 to 4 cups of sauce. Serve with lamb roast.

MEAT DISHES

VEAL "SWALLOW'S NESTS"

3 slices smoked raw ham (Westphalian type)
3 slices veal cutlets, cut from the leg
3 hard-boiled eggs, peeled
Salt and pepper
Flour for rolling
3 tablespoons butter
2 cups cubed soup vegetables (carrots, onion, celery)
1 cup light broth
2 tablespoons sour cream
Noodles cooked separately
1 teaspoon chopped parsley

1. Pound ham and veal slices so that they are large enough to enclose an egg. Roll first ham and then veal around each hard-boiled egg. Fasten with string or toothpick.
2. Season to taste with salt and pepper, and roll in flour. Brown each rolled egg on all sides in the butter.
3. Place in pot, accompanied by soup vegetables and broth. Cook until meat is soft, adding sour cream at end of cooking period.
4. Before serving, each rolled egg should be sliced in half horizontally, exposing the yolk, and placed on "nest" of cooked noodles, with cooking vegetables and sauce around it.

Garnish with parsley.

Makes 6 servings.

LITHUANIAN MEAT POCKETS
(Kolduny Litewskie)

Filling:

¼ pound bone marrow or suet
1 medium onion, grated
1 tablespoon butter
Salt and pepper
1 teaspoon marjoram
1 tablespoon bouillon
1 pound lean boneless lamb, chopped
4 cups clear bouillon, if serving as first course

Dough for meat pockets:

2 cups flour
1 extra large egg
A few teaspoons water as needed

Garnish:

Sour cream, served on the side
Fresh dill, chopped

1. Mash marrow to consistency of a purée.
2. Simmer onion in butter to a light golden brown. Add salt, pepper and marjoram, combine with marrow and moisten with bouillon. Blend thoroughly.
3. Combine with chopped lamb. (Some prefer to use ½ lamb and ½ beef, or even all beef, but I think all lamb tastes best). Roll mixture into small balls (⅓-inch round).
4. Prepare dough by mixing flour, egg and water together well. Work until firm. Roll into very thin sheet. Cut with a cookie cutter or glass, placing stuffing in center and folding over. Pinch edges securely. (May be frozen in single layer for later use.)

5. Cook pockets in a large pot of boiling water until they rise to the surface. Serve in clear bouillon, allowing 6 to 8 pockets per person. Sour cream and fresh chopped dill may be offered on the side.

The pockets may also be served as a luncheon dish. They should then be garnished with bread crumbs browned in melted butter.

Makes 4 to 5 servings.

 ## LITHUANIAN BEEF BIRDS

2 pounds beef (rump or bottom round), cut into slices
Salt and pepper
1 tablespoon flour for dredging
Butter for browning
1½ cups beef broth
½ cup sour cream

For filling:

2 medium onions
½ cup dried mushrooms, soaked in hot water
1 cup pumpernickel bread crumbs, divided
½ tablespoon butter
2 slices bacon, cubed
1 egg
1 teaspoon chopped parsley
Salt and pepper

1. Slice beef into thin pieces (⅛-inch). Pound lightly, sprinkle with salt and pepper to taste.
2. Prepare filling: finely chop onions and softened dried mushrooms. Add cup bread crumbs (saving 1 tablespoon

for sauce) and brown all three in butter. Add bacon, raw egg, parsley, and salt and pepper, mixing all well.

3. Place 2 to 3 tablespoons of filling on each slice of meat, roll up and secure with toothpick or string. Season with salt and pepper. Dip each piece in flour and brown in butter. Place browned "birds" in pot, pour broth around them and cook slowly under cover (about 1½ hours). When meat is soft, add sour cream mixed with 1 tablespoon bread crumbs saved from filling ingredient.

4. Remove string or toothpicks from the "birds," place on serving platter and pour the sauce in which they were cooked over them.

Serve with buckwheat groats.

Makes 8 to 10 servings.

 BOILED BEEF

3 to 4 pounds beef (rump, bottom round, shank, brisket, or plate)
Beef stock, commercial or home-made, enough to cover meat
Salt and pepper

1. Cover beef with cold stock. Bring to a boil and simmer very slowly for about 2 hours, or until meat is very tender but not falling apart. Remove meat and cool slightly before slicing. Reserve stock for use in sauces below.

2. Slice meat thin and serve with boiled potatoes and one of the following sauces:

Hot Horseradish Sauce:

1¼ tablespoons butter
2 tablespoons horseradish (freshly ground, if available)
1½ teaspoons flour
½ cup broth
1 cup sour cream
1½ teaspoons sugar (optional)
¼ teaspoon lemon juice
2 egg yolks (optional)

Melt butter without browning, add the horseradish and dust in the flour, stirring constantly until smooth, taking care not to brown. Dilute mixture slowly with the broth, and when well blended, add the sour cream, sugar, and lemon juice. Let boil up once and serve. If sugar is omitted the sauce will be sharper. If egg yolks are used (they are to be beaten and blended into the sauce slowly), the sauce will have a richer, subtler taste. Yields about 2 cups.

White Caper Sauce:

2 tablespoons butter
1 heaping tablespoon flour
1 cup broth
1 to 2 tablespoons chopped capers
½ teaspoon lemon juice and a little grated lemon rind
Salt
2 egg yolks

Melt butter and stir in flour, taking care not to brown. Blend well with broth. Chop and add capers, lemon juice and rind and season with salt to taste. (Seasoning will depend on the amount of capers used, since these are both salty and tangy.) Simmer for 10 minutes, and if too thick, dilute with more broth. When done, beat two egg yolks and add slowly, taking care not to let yolks curdle. Yields about 2 cups.

Makes 7 to 8 servings

MOCK VENISON POT ROAST

3 pounds beef, rump or eye round

Marinade to cover:

1 carrot, sliced
½ celery root, sliced
1 medium onion, sliced
20 peppercorns
10 juniper berries
1 bay leaf
Dash of thyme
Dash of marjoram
1 quart (4 cups) water
1½ to 2 cups red wine vinegar
Salt

Combine carrots, celery root, and onion with peppercorns, berries, bay leaf, thyme and marjoram and cook in water and vinegar for 30 minutes. Season with salt. Allow to cool. Add meat and let stand at least 24 hours, turning occasionally.

When ready to use, wipe meat dry and salt a half hour before cooking.

To pot-roast:

2 to 3 tablespoons butter
1 medium onion, diced
3 to 4 dried mushrooms
½ celery root, diced
A few sprigs parsley
Dash of thyme
Dash of marjoram
Salt and pepper
1 cup sour cream
1½ teaspoons flour

1. Brown meat on all sides in hot butter, using heavy skillet. Transfer to casserole.
2. Add onions, mushrooms, celery root, butter in which meat browned, parsley, thyme, marjoram, and salt and pepper to taste.
3. Simmer tightly covered, basting occasionally with cold water.
4. When tender—after about 2 hours—add sour cream blended with flour and simmer another 30 minutes.
5. Slice thin. Strain the sauce and pour over meat.

Makes 6 to 7 servings.

 ## HUSSAR POT ROAST

3 pounds beef, rump or eye round
2 cups marinade (as described in recipe for mock venison above), or 2 jiggers of vodka
2 to 3 tablespoons butter
2 medium onions, sliced
Salt and pepper

1. Blanch meat with boiling marinade; for a slightly blander taste, omit marinade and sprinkle meat with the vodka, having first browned it on all sides in hot butter. If using marinade, wipe meat off and brown as above.
2. Transfer to stock pot and simmer, tightly covered, together with the onions and butter in which meat was browned. Season with salt and pepper to taste. Sprinkle occasionally with cold water.
3. When meat is nearly tender—about 1½ to 2 hours—make the following stuffing:

Stuffing:

2 medium onions, blanched and grated
1 tablespoon bread crumbs
1 teaspoon butter
Salt and pepper

Mix all ingredients thoroughly. Slice the meat thin, taking care to make every second incision only part way. Fill these pockets with stuffing, reassemble into original shape, and return to stock pot.

Add:

1 tablespoon flour, dusted on top of meat
½ cup soup stock or a little more as needed.

Allow to simmer another 30 minutes.

Makes 6 to 7 servings.

 # BRIGANDS' POT ROAST

3 pounds boneless beef sirloin
2 tablespoons olive oil
3 to 4 medium onions, sliced
3 to 4 tablespoons butter
Salt and pepper
Flour for rolling, plus ½ teaspoon for sauce
3 to 4 tablespoons stock or bouillon
2 teaspoons caramelized sugar (recipe follows)

1. Rub the meat thoroughly with olive oil and cover all over with onion slices. Let stand at least 2 hours.

2. Half an hour before serving, heat the butter until brown, season the meat with salt and pepper, and roll in flour and sear quickly on both sides.
3. Add a few slices of the onion and allow them to brown. Add ½ teaspoon flour, soup stock and caramelized sugar.

Caramelized sugar:

Melt sugar in dry pan over low heat, and allow to caramelize until dark brown (taking care not to burn). Blend into stock.

4. When sauce is blended, put pot roast into hot oven for ten minutes, taking care not to overcook. Meat must be pink inside. Slice thin and pour sauce over meat.

Makes 6 to 7 servings.

 TRIPE

2 pounds tripe (honeycomb type)
2 carrots, diced
1 large onion, minced
1 celery root, diced
1 parsnip, diced
1 parsley root, diced
1 leek, cut fine
2 tablespoons butter
Soup stock or bouillon (about 2 cups) to cover
1 tablespoon flour
Dash of nutmeg
Dash of marjoram
1 teaspoon grated ginger
Salt and pepper
1 teaspoon Maggi extract or similar
½ cup milk

90

1. Soak tripe in cold water for several hours before using. Then cover tripe with fresh water, bring to a boil, drain and start again in cold water. When water begins to boil, cover and allow to simmer at least 2 hours.
2. Simmer vegetables in soup stock for 15 to 20 minutes.
3. Drain tripe, cut into thin strips and add to vegetables. The liquid should barely cover them.
4. Melt butter, combine with flour, stir until smooth and add to the pot. Simmer another 30 minutes.

The seasoning, especially the salt, should never be added before the last 30 minutes of cooking; otherwise the tripe will be tough and dark in color.

5. Add nutmeg, marjoram, ginger, salt and pepper, and Maggi extract 30 minutes before meat is done. Simmer tripe very slowly, tightly covered. For a light appearance, add milk.

May be served with suet or marrow balls, to which a lot of fresh dill has been added:

Suet or Marrow Balls:

¼ pound beef suet or marrow, or a mixture of the two
2 eggs, separated
Salt and pepper
2 tablespoons cracker meal or bread crumbs
1 tablespoon chopped fresh dill
Flour for rolling

1. Grind marrow or suet in processor or blender and cream with egg yolks, and salt and pepper to taste.
2. Add cracker meal and fold in beaten egg whites. Knead lightly with hands and shape into small balls, the size of a quarter in diameter.
3. Roll in flour and cook in boiling water for about 30 minutes. They are done when they rise to the surface.

Makes 8 servings.

LIVER PUDDING

2 pounds calf's liver
Milk or buttermilk for soaking
4 ounces salt pork for larding
Salt and pepper
Butter for browning
½ medium onion, chopped
3 to 4 tablespoons cold bouillon or water
2 to 3 tablespoons butter
6 eggs, separated
1 white roll moistened with milk and mashed
Dash of nutmeg
1 teaspoon grated lemon rind
Bread crumbs for lining

1. Soak liver in milk or buttermilk for 3 to 4 hours. Wipe, lard with thin strips of salt pork, and season with salt and pepper to taste just before putting into skillet.
2. Brown quickly on both sides in hot butter, adding the onion and taking care not to scorch either the meat or the onion. Reduce heat, cover and simmer for 15 minutes, basting with cold water or bouillon.
3. Allow liver to cool. Strain liquid in which it cooked. Reserve for later use.
4. Cut liver into small pieces, then purée in food processor or blender.
5. Cream butter and egg yolks, add strained meat sauce, mashed roll (bread crumbs may be substituted), salt, pepper, nutmeg, and lemon rind. Add liver and mix thoroughly. Fold in beaten egg whites last.
6. Pour into buttered mold which has been lined with bread crumbs. Cover tightly and place in a larger pan filled with water 2 inches high. Steam for 2 hours in 325-degree oven.

Serve with mushroom sauce, dill pickle sauce or any tangy sauce. Recipes follow.

Makes 5 to 6 servings.

Mushroom Sauce:

8 large fresh mushrooms
½ medium onion
2 tablespoons butter
1 tablespoon flour
Salt and pepper
1 cup broth
¼ cup white wine
2 to 3 tablespoons sweet cream
Lemon juice
2 egg yolks (optional)

1. Chop mushrooms, using both stems and caps. Chop onion fine, and sauté together with mushrooms in butter until onions are a golden brown and mushrooms soft (about 15 minutes).
2. Add flour and salt and pepper to taste and continue cooking, stirring constantly and taking care not to brown the flour, until thoroughly blended.
3. Slowly add the broth, and when sauce is smooth, add the wine and cream. Season with lemon juice to taste and simmer another 5 to 10 minutes.
4. For richer texture, add beaten egg yolks, taking care not to let them curdle. Serve at once.

Dill Pickle Sauce:

2 medium dill pickles
1 cup broth
1 tablespoon butter
1½ teaspoons flour
½ cup sour cream
Sugar

1. Peel pickles, slice thin, and simmer in broth 15 to 20 minutes.
2. Melt butter, add flour, and stir until smooth.
3. Combine with sour cream and slowly add the cucumbers and broth, stirring constantly until thoroughly blended. Let sauce boil up once. If it tastes too sour, add a pinch of sugar.

 ## SMOTHERED VEAL KIDNEYS

2 veal kidneys, with most of the fat removed
    (1 to 1½ pounds)
Flour for dredging, plus ½ teaspoon to mix with butter
2 to 3 tablespoons butter
½ cup bouillon
¼ cup sour cream
¼ teaspoon paprika
½ teaspoon marjoram
Lemon juice
Salt and pepper

1. Slice the kidneys diagonally, season and dust with flour. Brown quickly on both sides in hot butter. Set aside.
2. Using the butter in which kidneys browned, make a sauce as follows: Add ½ tablespoon flour to the butter and stir to a paste. Blend in bouillon, and add sour cream, paprika and marjoram. Season with lemon juice, and salt and pepper to taste.
3. Return kidneys to the sauce, cover tightly and simmer for about 10 minutes.

Makes 4 to 5 servings.

ROAST LAMB HUNTER-STYLE

1 leg of lamb (5 to 6 pounds), with bone
2 cups wine vinegar
20 juniper berries, pounded or ground
1 large clove garlic, mashed
1 large onion, sliced
¼ pound salt pork for larding
Salt and pepper
1 teaspoon butter
Flour for dredging
¼ cup sour cream

1. Remove excess fat from lamb, pound well and pour boiling vinegar over it. Rub well with juniper and garlic and surround with onion slices. Wrap in a cloth dipped in the vinegar and refrigerate 4 to 5 days.
2. Discard onion, wipe off meat, lard generously with salt pork, rub with salt and pepper and roast in hot oven (425 to 450 degrees) basting frequently for about 1¼ hours. When nearly done add sour cream, during the last 20 to 30 minutes of baking.

Makes 8 to 10 servings.

STUFFED ROAST LAMB

1 leg of lamb (5 to 6 pounds), boned
2 cups vinegar
Salt and pepper
1 large clove garlic, crushed
2 to 3 tablespoons butter
1 jigger pure alcohol or gin
1 to 2 medium carrots, diced
½ celery root, diced
1 parsley root, diced
2 celery stalks with leaves, diced
1 leek, diced
1 medium onion, diced
10 peppercorns
1 bay leaf
10 juniper berries
1 cup strong bouillon
Flour for dredging

For stuffing:

½ pound pork
½ pound veal
1 roll, moistened in milk and mashed
2 onions, grated and browned lightly in butter
2 egg yolks
Dash of nutmeg
1 teaspoon Maggi or Soy sauce
Salt and pepper

1. Pound meat well, remove excess fat and blanch with boiling vinegar. Wipe off and then rub with salt, pepper and garlic.
2. Make the stuffing as follows: grind pork, veal and roll in food processor or blender; add remaining ingredients

and mix thoroughly. Spread over inside of meat, roll tight, and tie securely.
3. Sear lamb in very hot butter. Sprinkle with alcohol. Add diced vegetables, onion and peppercorns, bay leaf and juniper berries. Add bouillon and simmer, tightly covered for 2½ hours.
4. When done, dust with flour, baste and let boil up once or twice. If necessary, add more stock as meat cooks, taking care not to make sauce too watery.

Makes 8 to 10 servings.

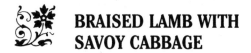 ## BRAISED LAMB WITH SAVOY CABBAGE

3 pounds breast of lamb
Salt for rubbing
1 clove garlic, mashed
1 medium onion, diced
Beef broth to cover
2 small heads Savoy cabbage, parboiled and cut in quarters
Salt and pepper
1 tablespoon butter
1 tablespoon flour

1. Rub meat with salt and garlic and allow to marinate 1 hour.
3. Put meat and onion in just enough beef broth to cover and simmer, skimming occasionally, for about 1 hour.
4. Remove meat, cut into serving pieces, and return to broth together with the parboiled cabbage. Season to taste and continue simmering, tightly covered, until meat and cabbage are thoroughly done.
5. Melt butter without browning, blend in the flour, and dissolve with some of the broth. Add to the pot. Allow to simmer until sauce thickens, another 15 minutes.

Makes 6 to 8 servings.

ROAST STUFFED SUCKLING PIG

1 whole suckling pig (10 to 12 pounds)
Salt for rubbing
1 stick (¼ pound) butter
A piece of salt pork or bacon, for rubbing
½ cup beer

1. Wash the pig well in cold water, dry and rub with salt inside and out an hour before stuffing. (Recipes for two stuffings follow.) Sew together or secure with skewers.
2. Arrange pig on its stomach in a roasting pan, rub well with butter and roast in a 450-degree oven at first; after 40 minutes reduce to 350 degrees.
3. Roast pig will taste best if the skin is browned fast. It should crackle when done. To that end the roast should be basted very frequently, first with the pan drippings, which will be mostly butter, then (after it has begun to brown) with beer. Alternate the basting with beer with rubbing the skin with a piece of salt pork or bacon on a stick.
4. The total roasting time is 2½ to 3 hours. To test doneness, try meat with a fork where it is thickest; if watery liquid comes out, the meat is still raw; if fat oozes out, the meat is done. The skin should by then be a good orange color, but care must be taken not to burn it.

Makes 12 to 15 servings.

Stuffings for Roast Pig:

Liver Pâté Stuffing:

1 large onion
1 carrot
1 to 2 stalks celery
½ celery root
½ parsley root
A few sprigs parsley
1 parsnip
Pork liver (from your suckling pig)
Pork lungs (from your suckling pig)
1 pound boneless veal, ground
2 tablespoons butter
10 peppercorns
Salt and pepper
2 stale rolls moistened in milk and mashed, or equivalent
    in moistened bread crumbs
Dash of nutmeg
2 whole eggs
¼ pound salt pork or bacon

1. Peel and cut onion, carrot, celery, celery root, parsley root, parsley, and parsnip. Combine with all the meats.
2. Add butter, peppercorns, and salt and pepper to taste. Simmer, tightly covered, with a very small amount of water. The liver will be done in 15 to 20 minutes. Lungs and veal will take longer.
3. When done, process everything. Combine mixture with mashed rolls, nutmeg and two whole eggs. (For a lighter stuffing eggs may be separated, the egg whites beaten and folded in last.)
4. Add the liquid in which meat was simmered, and the bacon or salt pork, diced fine. Mix well and stuff.

Buckwheat Groats Stuffing:

1 cup whole buckwheat groats, cooked separately
(recipe below)
Liver, lungs, and kidney from the pig
¼ pound bacon or salt pork
2 medium onions, chopped fine and smothered in butter,
but not browned
1 whole egg
Salt and pepper
Dash of nutmeg
¼ teaspoon marjoram
½ cup strong bouillon

1. Prepare buckwheat groats according to recipe below.
2. Chop meat and bacon fine; combine with smothered onions, egg, salt and pepper, nutmeg, and marjoram.
3. Add to groats and mix thoroughly.
4. Moisten with bouillon and stuff the pig.

Buckwheat Groats:

1. Break a whole egg into one cup of whole buckwheat groats.
2. Heat on a dry frying pan, stirring, until each grain becomes separate.
3. All at once, add 2 cups of boiling water, and cook for about 20 minutes tightly covered.
4. Add salt (½ to 1 teaspoon) after cooking. (You may also add hot broth instead of water, in which case salt may not be needed.)

STUFFED SAVOY CABBAGE

2 small heads Savoy cabbage
Salted boiling water
1 medium onion, minced
1 tablespoon butter
1 pound ground meat (beef, pork or lamb, as well as
    left-over roast, according to preference)
1 white roll, moistened in milk and mashed (or 1 cup
    cooked rice)
Salt
Pepper
Dash of nutmeg
2 whole eggs, lightly beaten
Bacon strips for lining

1. Parboil cabbage for 5 minutes in salted boiling water.
   Drain and cool.
2. Spread cooled cabbage leaves, cut out the hard center of
   each leaf and fill with the following stuffing: Brown onion
   lightly in butter. Mix thoroughly with meat, roll (or rice),
   salt, pepper, nutmeg, and eggs.
3. Roll up each filled leaf and arrange tightly in a casserole
   lined with bacon strips. Extra pieces of cabbage may be
   tucked into corners of casserole.
4. Add ½ cup of water or broth, a small can (6 to 8 ounces)
   of tomatoes (or two sliced fresh tomatoes) and cover
   tightly.
5. Bake covered in a 375-degree oven for about 1½ hours,
   until cabbage looks baked and brown.

This may be done a day earlier and reheated before serving.

Just before serving, add sauce: combine 1 tablespoon
butter, 1½ teaspoons flour, ½ cup of sour cream and ½ cup
of water or bouillon and boil.

Makes 8 to 10 servings.

ROAST BEEF GYPSY STYLE

1 loin beef roast (4 pounds)
2 slices bacon, sliced fine
Salt and pepper
2 large yellow onions, chopped fine
1 tablespoon paprika
Pinch of cayenne pepper
½ teaspoon ground allspice
½ teaspoon ground cloves
2 cups beef broth, divided
6 tablespoons butter

Preheat oven to 400 degrees.

1. Using a small paring knife, cut incisions in the beef and push a slice of bacon in each. Season meat with salt and pepper to taste. Place the beef in a large roasting pan, with chopped onions around it. Sprinkle onions on the roast with the paprika, cayenne, allspice and cloves.
2. Pour about 1 cup of the broth into the pan. Arrange the butter on top of the meat and place pan in the oven.
3. After 15 minutes, baste the meat and reduce oven temperature to 350 degrees. Continue roasting, basting occasionally, and adding more broth if needed, for a total of 2 hours (about 30 minutes per pound).
4. Remove the roast to a serving platter and keep warm in the oven (set to "warm").
5. The sauce should be quite thick. You may wish to increase its volume by adding some more broth and boiling it quickly on top of the stove.
6. Slice roast and pour sauce over it.

Makes 6 to 7 servings.

ROAST BEEF IN DILL SAUCE

3 to 4-pound sirloin tip roast
2 slices bacon, sliced fine
Salt and pepper
6 tablespoons butter, divided
1 cup dry white wine
2 tablespoons flour
3 tablespoons chopped fresh dill
Zest of 1 lemon
1 cup heavy cream

Preheat oven to 400 degrees.

1. Using a small paring knife, lard the roast with pieces of bacon. Season with salt and pepper to taste.
2. Put the roast in a roasting pan, place 3 tablespoons of the butter on top and pour on the white wine. Place in the oven and roast for 15 minutes.
3. Baste and turn the oven down to 350 degrees. Continue roasting, basting occasionally and adding a bit of water if necessary to prevent burning, until tender, about another 1½ hours.
4. Transfer roast to a serving platter and place in warm oven.
5. Skim off any excess fat from the pan juices and add some water to make a cup of liquid. Melt the remaining butter in a frying pan, then stir in the flour and fry for 2 minutes.
6. Stir in the pan juices and bring to a low boil on top of the stove.
7. Add the dill and grated lemon zest and season with additional salt and pepper, to taste. Cook for another 2 minutes.
8. Stir in the cream and heat through.

Pour sauce over roast and serve.

Makes 5 to 6 servings.

ROAST VEAL WITH WILD MUSHROOMS AND GARLIC

1 ounce dried porcini mushrooms
OR
6 ounces fresh wild mushrooms (which are now widely available)
3-pound rolled veal loin
2 cloves garlic, sliced thin
Salt and pepper
1 teaspoon marjoram
2 tablespoons olive or vegetable oil
1 cup dry white wine
1 cup broth if using fresh mushrooms
4 tablespoons butter, divided
2 tablespoons flour
2 tablespoons fresh chopped parsley or dill

1. If using dried mushrooms, place them in 1 cup of warm water to soak for about 20 minutes. Drain, reserving the liquid. Chop mushrooms roughly. If using fresh mushrooms, cut in strips and reserve for later use.

Preheat oven to 350 degrees.

2. Using a small paring knife, cut incisions in the roast and insert a small slice of garlic in each. Season well with salt and pepper. Rub in the marjoram.
3. Heat the oil in a large frying pan on medium heat. When pan is quite hot, put in the veal and brown well on all sides.
4. Place the veal in a small roasting pan and pour the wine around it. Add the mushrooms and their liquid. If using fresh mushrooms, add 1 cup of broth instead.
5. Put 2 tablespoons of the butter over the meat. Place the roast in the oven. Cook, basting occasionally, for 2 hours.

6. Remove the veal to a serving platter and keep warm. Skim off any excess fat from the pan juices.
7. Melt the remaining butter in a frying pan, then stir in the flour and fry for 3 minutes. Add the pan juices and let boil, stirring well, for another 2 minutes. Season to taste and add the fresh parsley or dill.

Makes 5 to 6 servings.

 ## VEAL STEW WITH MUSHROOMS

1½ pounds stewing veal, cut into ½-inch pieces
2 tablespoons flour for dredging
2 tablespoons butter
1 medium onion, chopped
2 cloves garlic, crushed
¾ pound mushrooms, sliced thick (ordinary white mushrooms will do, although a tastier mushroom such as the portobello or shitake will make the stew even better)
1 cup dry white wine
Juice of 1 lemon
4 cups water
½ teaspoon marjoram
Salt and pepper
2 tablespoons fresh chopped parsley or dill
½ cup sour cream

1. Pour boiling water over veal (to prevent juices from seeping out) and dry with paper towels. Dredge veal pieces in flour.
2. Heat the butter in a large pot and put in the coated veal to brown lightly on all sides.
3. Add the chopped onion and fry, stirring occasionally, until almost golden. Add crushed garlic.

4. Add the mushrooms and brown them.
5. Add the white wine, lemon juice and about 4 cups of water. Stir in the marjoram and season with salt and pepper to taste. Add chopped parsley or dill. Cover the pot and bring to a low boil. Reduce the heat and simmer until the meat is tender, about 1½ hours.
6. Stir in sour cream shortly before serving (mixed with a bit of flour if sauce is too watery).

Makes 4 to 5 servings.

 ## BEEF WITH CELERIAC

1 pound sirloin
Salt and pepper
4 tablespoons butter, divided
1 medium onion, chopped
2 cups beef broth
½ small celeriac, cut into fine strips
2 tablespoons chopped dill
2 tablespoons flour
½ cup sour cream

1. Trim the fat from the sirloin and slice the meat across the grain into strips about ¼-inch thick. Season the beef with salt and pepper to taste.
2. Heat 2 tablespoons of the butter in a large frying pan. When pan is quite hot, add the beef and brown.
3. Add the onion and fry, stirring occasionally, until almost golden. Add the broth and check seasonings. Bring to a boil, reduce the heat and simmer, uncovered, for about 20 minutes.
4. Meanwhile, bring a small pot of salted water to a brisk boil. Put in the julienned celeriac and cook until tender, about 5 minutes. Drain.

5. Add celeriac to the beef. Stir in the chopped dill.
6. To thicken the sauce, make a roux by melting the remaining butter in a small frying pan, adding the flour and cooking for about 3 to 4 minutes. Stir the roux into the beef sauce mixture and cook for a couple of minutes longer.
7. Just before serving, mix in the sour cream and heat the sauce through.

Makes 4 servings.

 ## VEAL WITH LEEKS

4 small to medium leeks
3 tablespoons butter
1½ pounds stewing veal, cut into ½-inch cubes
1 clove garlic, crushed
2 tablespoons flour
2 cups beef broth
Juice of 1 lemon
½ teaspoon thyme
Salt and pepper
½ cup heavy cream
1 egg yolk (optional)

1. Cut off the ends of the leeks, discard their green parts, and cut them in half. Wash them well under running water (they have lots of sand hidden in their little crevices) and slice them thinly.
2. Melt the butter in a large frying pan over medium heat. When it is hot, add the veal and brown it on all sides.
3. Add the sliced leeks and garlic and fry for 3 to 4 minutes, stirring occasionally.

4. Stir in the flour and continue cooking for 2 to 3 minutes. Add the broth, lemon juice and thyme. Season to taste with salt and pepper. Bring to a low boil, reduce the heat and simmer until tender, for about 45 minutes, partially covered.
5. Stir in the heavy cream (mixed with egg yolk, if using) just before serving and heat through on low heat.

Makes 4 servings.

 ## VEAL TONGUE WITH MUSTARD AND CAPERS

Veal tongue has a very delicate taste that is unfamiliar to many Americans. It is well worth trying.

1 fresh (not smoked) veal tongue (2 pounds)
Salt and pepper
2 tablespoons butter
1 small onion, finely chopped
2 tablespoons flour
2 cups beef broth
2 tablespoons mustard
1 teaspoon marjoram
1 tablespoon chopped fresh parsley
Juice of 1 lemon
1 tablespoon capers

1. Cover the tongue with cold water and sprinkle in some salt. Bring to a boil and simmer, covered, until it is tender, about 1½ hours.
2. Remove the tongue from its liquid and let cool a little. Peel off the skin of the tongue and leave to cool further.
3. When the tongue is completely cool, slice it diagonally into ½-inch slices. Set aside until sauce is ready.

To make sauce:

1. Melt the butter in a large frying pan on medium heat. Once it starts bubbling, add the onion and fry, stirring occasionally, until it is almost golden. Mix in the flour and fry for 2 more minutes.
2. Pour in the broth, mixing well, and bring to a low boil. Stir in the mustard. Add the marjoram, parsley, lemon juice and capers. Season to taste.
3. Add the tongue slices to the sauce and heat through for about 5 minutes.

Makes 4 servings.

 LAMB BRAISED WITH ONIONS

3 pounds lamb shoulder (or leg of lamb)
2 tablespoons butter
3 large onions, finely chopped
2 cloves garlic, crushed
2 tablespoons flour
2 cups dry white wine
4 cloves
1 teaspoon marjoram
2 tablespoons fresh chopped parsley
2 tablespoons mustard
1 lemon (grated rind and juice)
Salt and pepper
A little flour to thicken

Preheat the oven to 350 degrees.

1. Trim off any excess fat and tie the roast to keep it in place.

2. Heat the butter in a large dutch oven (that is oven safe) and brown meat on all sides after the surface becomes hot. Remove the meat from the pot and set aside, skimming off any excess fat.
3. Add the onions to the pot and lower the heat to medium-low. Fry until almost golden. Add the garlic and fry another 2 minutes or so. Sprinkle on the flour and cook another couple of minutes.
4. Place the meat back in the pot. Pour on the wine and about 2 cups of water. Add the cloves, marjoram, parsley, and mustard.
5. Grate the peel of the lemon into the sauce and then squeeze in the juice. Add salt and pepper to taste. Cover and place in the oven. Cook for about 2½ hours, turning the meat over once or twice.
6. Once the lamb is tender, the onions should be fairly well dissolved and the sauce not runny; if not, you may mash the onions with a fork or potato masher and thicken the sauce with a bit of flour mixed in water.
7. Slice the lamb and cover with sauce.

Makes 5 to 6 servings.

VENISON MEDALLIONS IN RED WINE

1½ pounds venison tenderloin
Salt and pepper
4 tablespoons butter, divided
1 small onion, finely chopped
2 cloves garlic, crushed
1 cup dry red wine
1 tablespoon fresh chopped parsley

1. Slice the venison into medallions about ¾-inch thick and rub them with black pepper.
2. Heat 2 tablespoons of the butter in a frying pan over medium-high heat. When quite hot, add the medallions and fry them until golden brown on both sides.
3. Reduce the heat to medium and add the onion and garlic. Fry for a couple of minutes more.
4. Add the red wine and raise the heat to high.
5. Remove the meat and keep in a warm place.
6. Boil the sauce quickly and reduce by about half. Adjust the seasonings, and add chopped parsley.

Venison is usually served medium or medium-rare, unless you prefer well done. If you do, cook a meat a bit longer before removing to warming platter.

Makes 4 servings.

PORK FILLET ROULADE

1 pork fillet (2 to 3 pounds)
Salt and pepper
1 pound ground veal
½ pound calves liver, chopped
1 egg
2 tablespoons bread crumbs
1 medium onion, chopped
1 tablespoon butter
2 medium carrots, sliced

1. Cut pork fillet into a flat shape, preparing it for stuffing. Rub with salt and pepper.
2. Combine veal, liver, egg, bread crumbs, onion (which has first been sautéed in the butter), and salt and pepper to taste. Mix well. The mixture will be solid.
3. Spread the stuffing on the prepared pork, roll and wrap in cheese cloth.
4. Place meat in a pot, cover with the carrots and add two cups of hot water. Cover pot tightly and braise for 1½ to 2 hours.
5. When the cooking is completed, cool and press the pork, without removing it from the broth. When completely cool, remove the cheese cloth.
6. Cut into thin slices on a platter and serve cold with horseradish.

Makes 6 to 8 servings.

SMOKED HAM BAKED IN DOUGH

1 smoked ham (5 to 6 pounds), outer skin off
Flour for sprinkling
Pepper
Caraway seeds
Rye bread dough (recipe follows)
1 piece bacon fat for rubbing

Preheat oven to 425 degrees.

1. Sprinkle the ham with a bit of flour, pepper, and caraway seeds to taste.
2. Cover with the prepared dough to a thickness of one finger. Wet your hands with cold water, and smooth out the surface of the dough.
3. Place the ham in a roasting pan and bake for 3 to 3½ hours in a 425-degree oven.
4. Cool slightly, and remove the dough covering, scraping it off completely. Rub the skin of the ham with bacon fat for a nice shine, and put it back into the oven for 5 to 10 minutes to dry the surface.

Makes 10 to 12 servings.

Rye Bread Dough:

6 cups rye flour
2 cups warm water
1 ounce yeast (or sourdough starter)
½ teaspoon sugar

1. Mix ⅓ of the flour with warm water and add the yeast mixed with sugar. Sprinkle the top of the mixture with flour, cover with a cloth, and put in a warm place to rise.
2. After the dough has risen, add the remaining flour. Knead until it is smooth. Let stand and rise again.

Makes 10 to 12 servings.

HAM AND BREAD CASSEROLE

¾ pound rye or pumpernickel bread
4 eggs, separated
2 tablespoons butter, divided
½ cup sour cream
Salt and pepper
½ pound ham, cut into julienne strips
2 medium onions, grated
Bread crumbs for sprinkling
2 tablespoons grated cheese for sprinkling

Preheat the oven to 350 degrees.

1. Soak the bread in a little water, squeeze it out, and place in a bowl. Beat with a wooden spoon, adding one egg yolk at a time, until all four yolks are incorporated.
2. Then add 1 tablespoon of the butter, the sour cream, salt and pepper to taste, and the beaten egg whites. Mix lightly.
3. Sauté the julienned ham and grated onion in the remaining butter.
4. Butter a casserole dish and sprinkle with bread crumbs.
5. Place a layer of the dough (one finger thick) on the bottom of the dish, and add a layer of the ham mixture of the same thickness. Continue, alternating the layers until the dough and the ham mixture are used up, with a dough layer on top. Sprinkle with grated cheese.
6. Bake at 350 degrees for 20 to 25 minutes, or until golden in color.

May be served with a tomato-onion sauce. (Recipe follows.)

114

Tomato-Onion Sauce:

½ tablespoon flour
2 tablespoons olive oil
1 medium onion, grated
2 tablespoons thick tomato paste (or 2 fresh ripe
    tomatoes, puréed)
Salt
Pepper
Vinegar
Sugar

1. Sauté the flour in olive oil until browned. Add grated onion and tomato paste and sauté again.
2. Dilute with hot water, mixing constantly to make a smooth texture.
3. Add salt, pepper, vinegar, and sugar and bring to a boil. Add a bit of water again if sauce is too thick. It should be slightly runny.

Makes 4 to 5 servings.

 ## BRAISED BEEF WITH HORSERADISH STUFFING

1 beef roast (2 to 2½ pounds), rump or sirloin tip
Salt and pepper
2 tablespoons butter
1 medium onion, sliced
2 bay leaves
2 medium carrots, sliced
1 stalk celery, sliced
A small bunch of parsley leaves
1 leek, sliced
1 cup broth

1. Pound the meat lightly, rub with salt and pepper to taste. Brown on all sides in hot butter and add the onion, bay leaves, carrots, celery, parsley, leek, and broth. Braise over low heat. Add extra broth if you see that the meat is adhering to the bottom of the pot.
2. About halfway through the cooking (after about 1 hour), make slits in the meat in several places, stuff with horseradish mixture (recipe follows), and continue braising until the meat is tender.
3. Serve sliced, with sauce made from the cooking liquid which has been strained.

Horseradish Stuffing:

2 tablespoons butter
1 tablespoon bread crumbs
½ cup grated horseradish (either fresh or bottled)
1 tablespoon sugar
2 egg yolks
Juice of 1 lemon
Salt and pepper

1. Melt the butter in a small pot, add bread crumbs, horseradish, sugar, beaten egg yolks, lemon juice, and salt and pepper to taste. Mix while heating.
2. Stuff the meat with this mixture about halfway through its cooking, putting stuffing into slits made in the meat.

Makes 6 to 8 servings.

INDIVIDUAL MEAT LOAVES

3 tablespoons bread crumbs
1 medium onion, grated
½ cup sour cream
Salt and pepper
2 pounds lean chopped beef
½ pound suet, finely chopped
1 tablespoon butter
2 tablespoons butter for frying

1. Add bread crumbs, onion, sour cream, and salt and pepper to taste to the beef. Add the chopped suet and knead. Mixture should be soft.

Preheat oven to 375 degrees.

2. Wet your hands with cold water and shape mixture into round, slightly flattened meat loaves.
3. Fry the loaves in hot butter until they are nicely browned, and immediately put them into the oven for 10 minutes, where they will swell up. These meat loaves made without egg are softer and tastier than the others, but they must be evenly shaped. Their surface should not contain any openings, to prevent bursting while they are frying.

Makes 6 to 8 servings.

LITHUANIAN STEW

2 pounds lean beef for stew
2 tablespoons flour for dredging
4 tablespoons butter
1 medium onion, sliced
3 medium carrots, sliced
2 stalks celery, sliced
1 leek, sliced
1 parsnip, sliced
1 bay leaf
2 cups broth
½ cup sour cream
Salt and pepper

1. Cut beef into fairly large pieces, pound, sprinkle with flour, and brown in hot butter.
2. Place a layer of coarsely sliced onion, carrots, celery, leek, parsnip, and bay leaf in a heavy pot, add a layer of meat, then vegetables, until all the vegetables and meat are used up. The top layer should be vegetables.
3. Add the broth, cover the pot tightly, and braise until the meat is tender (about 2 hours).
4. Add the sour cream and salt and pepper to taste. Heat through.

This stew is usually served with broad egg noodles.

Makes 5 to 6 servings.

BOILED BEEF WITH CHEESE

1 boneless beef roast (3 pounds), rump or sirloin tip
4 cups beef broth (reserve 1 cup for sauce)
1 medium onion, chopped
3 tablespoons butter
1 tablespoon flour
1 cup sour cream
2 egg yolks
Salt and pepper
3 tablespoons grated Swiss or other yellow cheese

1. Braise the meat in boiling broth until it becomes tender, usually about 2 hours. Reserve 1 cup of the broth.

Preheat oven to 450 degrees.

2. Remove the meat from the liquid, cool, slice, and arrange in a casserole dish.
3. Sauté the onion in butter, add the flour, brown slightly. Stir in the sour cream and one cup of the reserved broth.
4. Bring to a boil and beat in the egg yolks, add salt and pepper to taste, and pour over the meat.
5. Sprinkle with the grated cheese and place into a 450-degree oven to brown (for about 15 minutes).

Makes 6 to 7 servings.

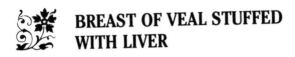 **BREAST OF VEAL STUFFED WITH LIVER**

1 breast of veal (3 to 4 pounds)
1 pound liver (calves' or beef)
½ pound bacon, chopped
2 medium onions, chopped
1 leek, finely chopped
Salt and pepper
2 cups broth (reserve 1 cup for basting)
1 egg
A bit of milk or cream
2 tablespoons butter

1. Using a sharp knife, make a pocket between the bones and the meat in the veal breast.

Preheat the oven to 375 degrees.

Prepare the stuffing as follows:

1. Cut the liver into small pieces and place into a pot. Add the bacon, onion, leek, and salt and pepper to taste, and braise for a few minutes.
2. Cover the mixture with broth and braise for 20 to 30 minutes. Cool.
3. Grind the mixture thoroughly in a blender or food processor.
4. Beat in the egg and a bit of milk or cream if the consistency seems too stiff or dry. Stir well.
5. Stuff the veal breast with this mixture, sew or skewer the pocket and roast in a 375-degree oven for about 1½ to 2 hours, basting with butter and broth occasionally.

Carve into portions along the bones.

Makes 5 to 6 servings.

CABBAGE MEAT PIE
(Plauciu Kepsnys)

1 medium onion, chopped
1 stick butter
1 medium cabbage, shredded
Salt
Nutmeg
Pepper
1 cup ground left-over beef or veal
2 hard-boiled eggs, chopped
1 cup sliced mushrooms
Butter or shortening for greasing pie pan
Pastry for a 9-inch pie with top layer

Preheat oven to 400 degrees.

1. Sauté the onion in butter. Add shredded cabbage and salt to taste. Cook on a low flame until cabbage is tender, about 20 minutes.
2. Season the ground meat with nutmeg, and salt and pepper to taste. Add the meat, chopped eggs, and mushrooms to the cabbage. Cook for about 5 minutes.
3. Grease a pie pan with butter, and line with pastry dough. Spoon in the cabbage and meat mixture. Cover with pastry dough.
4. Bake for 25 to 30 minutes, or until the top is brown.

Makes 5 to 6 servings.

VEAL FRICASSEE WITH DILL SAUCE

2 pounds veal for stew, cut into about 1-inch pieces
2 cups beef broth
2 tablespoons butter
2 tablespoons flour
½ cup sour cream
3 tablespoons finely chopped fresh dill
Salt and pepper

1. Pour boiling, salted water over the veal, drain, and rinse. (This keeps the juices from running out; another way is to sear in fat on all sides, as in the following recipe.)
2. Place the veal in a pot with 2 cups of broth. After the meat comes to a boil, skim and continue cooking covered until the meat is tender.
3. Brown the butter with the flour and add the broth that the meat cooked in to make a sauce.
4. Add the sour cream, dill, and salt and pepper to taste. Pour the sauce over the meat. Heat through before serving.

Makes 5 to 6 servings.

GRATINATED VEAL ROAST

1½ pounds boneless veal fillet
7 tablespoons butter, divided
1½ cups beef broth
2 tablespoons flour
1 cup milk
½ cup sour cream
2 egg yolks
2 tablespoons grated cheese
1½ tablespoons bread crumbs

1. Brown the veal in 2 tablespoons of the butter on all sides. Add the broth and cook under cover until the meat becomes tender, turning several times. This should take 1 to 1½ hours. Cool the meat completely, as it then becomes much easier to slice.

Preheat oven to 425 degrees.

2. Slice into thin pieces and arrange on an oven-proof deep platter.
3. Melt 3 tablespoons of the butter in a pan, add the flour, and brown slightly. Add the milk and sour cream, stirring to prevent lumps. Add the liquid from the veal.
4. Add the yolks to the sauce slowly, and pour over the meat platter.
5. Top with the grated cheese (Swiss or similar), the remaining melted butter, and the bread crumbs.
6. Bake for 20 to 25 minutes, until the cheese melts and becomes golden in color.

Makes 5 to 6 servings.

ROAST PORK LOIN WITH PRUNES

2 pounds pork loin
Salt
Flour for rolling (about 2 tablespoons)
3 tablespoons butter, oil, or shortening
1½ cups pitted prunes

Preheat oven to 350 degrees.

1. Sprinkle pork with salt to taste. Roll in flour and brown in butter on all sides. Transfer to a baking dish, adding the fat the meat had browned in and 3 to 4 tablespoons water. Bake in a 350-degree oven. Baste occasionally with butter, adding a bit of water if needed.
2. When the pork is about halfway done (about 45 minutes), add the prunes and continue baking, basting, and adding a little water from time to time, letting the prunes plump up in the oven.
3. Slice the roast into thin pieces, decorate with the prunes around the edges and pour the roasting liquid over it.

Makes 5 to 6 servings.

LAMB ROAST WITH SAVOY CABBAGE

1½ pounds of lamb, leg portion
1 clove garlic
Flour for rolling
5 tablespoons butter, shortening, or oil, divided
1 small (about 1 pound) head Savoy cabbage, quartered
1 tablespoon caraway seeds
3 tablespoons flour (for sauce)
Salt and pepper
Vinegar
Sugar

1. Remove the lamb from its bones (if any) and take off any excess fat. Pound the meat with a pestle, rub it with garlic and roll in flour.
2. Brown on all sides in 2 tablespoons of the hot butter in a pan. Remove the meat to a pot, adding ½ cup of water. Simmer, covered, until the meat is almost tender (usually about 60 minutes), adding a bit of water when it evaporates.
3. Remove the tough outer leaves of the cabbage, and then rinse and quarter it.
4. Take the lamb out of the pot, let it cool a bit to facilitate carving, and cut into medium slices against the grain of the meat.
5. Place the meat back into the pot, layering it with the cabbage (cabbage is top layer). Sprinkle each layer with caraway seeds. Add another ½ cup of water and continue braising until completely tender.
6. Melt the remaining butter in a pan, add the flour, dilute the mixture with a little water and pour into the pot. Heat through and add salt, pepper, vinegar, and sugar to taste.

Makes 4 to 5 servings.

BEEF FILLET À LA NELSON

Preheat oven to 450 degrees.

¼ cup dried mushrooms
1½ pounds beef fillet
Flour to dust, plus 1 tablespoon
3 tablespoons butter
5 medium potatoes, peeled and cut into medium slices
½ cup onion, sliced
Salt and pepper
½ cup sour cream

1. Soak the mushrooms in hot water until they become soft (about 30 minutes). Remove from their liquid and cut into thin strips. Reduce the liquid by boiling to ½ cup. Set aside for later use.
2. Cut the beef into 8 to 10 slices, depending on the exact size of the meat, to a thickness of about ½-inch. Dust with flour and quickly brown in hot butter (so that they remain pink inside). Set aside.
3. Cook the potato slices until they are half done. Drain.
4. Brown the onion in the butter the meat was cooked in.
5. Using a flat pan or oven-proof platter, arrange the meat pieces, alternating with the potatoes, onion, and mushrooms. Add salt and pepper to taste.
6. Pour over the sour cream, mixed with the remaining tablespoon of flour and the reserved mushroom liquid. Cover tightly with a lid or piece of foil and bake at 450 degrees for 10 to 15 minutes.

Makes 4 to 5 servings.

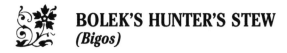

BOLEK'S HUNTER'S STEW
(Bigos)

This traditional dish, enjoyed by hunters and others inhabiting country mansions during the previous century, takes three days to complete, but it is well worth waiting for!

Ingredients for day 1:

2 pounds sauerkraut
2 to 3 pounds pork roast
1 to 2 teaspoons caraway seeds
2 to 3 bay leaves

Stew sauerkraut with pork roast, caraway seeds and bay leaves for 3 hours on medium heat, making sure that there is a little bit of water in the pot at all times.

Ingredients for day 2:

1 medium cabbage, shredded
½ cup dried mushrooms, softened in hot water and cut into small strips (liquid from mushrooms is then added to stew along with mushrooms)
1 medium can (1 pound) of stewed tomatoes or equivalent in fresh
2 sour apples (such as Granny Smith), sliced thin

Add all of these to first day's ingredients and stew for about two hours more.

Ingredients for day 3:

2 envelopes (.14 ounce each) beef broth powder
(or 2 teaspoons beef base such as Knorr's Gourmet
Edge Beef Base)
1 teaspoon sugar
1 to 1½ cups dry red wine
1 pound Polish sausage, cut into slices
[other possible additions can be pieces of roast duck, cold
cooked meats, (beef or veal) cut into strips, or other
types of sausage]

Continue cooking with new additions for another hour or so.

This dish becomes better each time it is reheated.

Makes 15 to 20 servings.

POULTRY &
GAME DISHES

DUCK BRAISED IN RED CABBAGE

1 duckling (about 5 pounds)
Butter for basting
1 medium red cabbage
Salt and pepper
Juice of ½ lemon
2 to 3 ounces salt pork or bacon, diced
1 small onion
2 teaspoons flour
1 cup red wine
1 teaspoon sugar
1 tablespoon caraway seeds

1. Prepare duck and salt it 2 hours in advance.
2. Roast in 425-degree oven, basting frequently with butter, until nicely brown (30 to 40 minutes).
3. In the meantime, shred the cabbage, blanch with boiling water, and drain. Season with salt and pepper to taste and sprinkle with lemon juice. Juice helps preserve the bright red color.
4. In a heavy pot, brown the diced salt pork or bacon and onion lightly, add flour, and stir to keep from lumping.
5. Add cabbage, red wine, sugar, and caraway seeds. Simmer, tightly covered.
6. When duck is brown, transfer to the pot with the cabbage, adding the butter and duck fat from the roasting pan. Let simmer, covered, until thoroughly done—about one more hour.

Makes 3 to 4 servings.

SQUAB PREPARED AS GAME BIRDS

4 squabs
1 tablespoon crushed juniper berries
Salt pork or bacon for larding
Salt and pepper
2 to 3 strips bacon, diced
1 medium onion, sliced
1 carrot, diced
1 leek, diced
1 to 2 celery stalks, diced
Pieces of celery root and parsley root if available, diced
10 peppercorns
1 bay leaf
Pinch of thyme
Pinch of marjoram
1 cup dry red wine
1 tablespoon bread crumbs
3 to 4 tablespoons sour cream

1. Prepare squabs a day ahead of time: rub with juniper inside and out.
2. One hour before cooking, lard squabs generously and rub with salt and pepper. Arrange in heavy pot or casserole, together with diced bacon, onion and diced vegetables. Add peppercorns, bay leaf, thyme and marjoram, and additional salt and pepper to taste, and a little of the wine. Cover tightly and simmer about 15 minutes.
3. Add bread crumbs and continue simmering, adding wine a little at a time, until done (30 to 35 minutes).
4. Press sauce and vegetables through sieve or food mill, return to pot to heat, add sour cream and let bubble up once. Pour over squabs.

Makes 4 servings.

EMPEROR CASSEROLE OF CAPON

Capon or chicken (4 to 5 pounds)
Salt and pepper
2 tablespoons butter
12 shallots or small white onions
6 medium mushrooms, sliced or quartered
1 to 2 truffles, sliced thin (optional)
1 cup bouillon
1 cup red wine
2 teaspoons butter (for sauce)
2 teaspoons flour
½ teaspoon Maggi extract (or similar)

1. Clean capon and rub with salt and pepper 1 hour ahead of time.
2. Cut in serving pieces and brown lightly in butter in a stock pot in which it is to cook.
3. Add peeled shallots, mushrooms and truffles. Season to taste and simmer, tightly covered, for about 30 minutes.
4. Add bouillon and wine and continue simmering until done (20 to 30 minutes more).
5. Melt butter to a light-brown color, blend in flour, add enough of the liquid to blend thoroughly and use to thicken sauce. Add Maggi extract, allow to bubble up and pour over meat.

Makes 4 to 5 servings.

DUCK AND RICE CASSEROLE

1 duckling (about 5 pounds), cut in serving pieces
1 medium onion
Enough chicken broth to cover
2 cups uncooked rice
Salt and pepper
Grated Parmesan
1 cup sour cream

1. Cook duckling with onion in 4 to 5 cups of broth, skimming carefully, simmering until done (about 1½ hours).
2. Strain liquid and use to cook rice as follows: Pour boiling bouillon over rice, cover and let stand 10 minutes. Season to taste with salt and pepper.
3. In a heavy, greased casserole, arrange rice and duck in layers, sprinkling each layer with Parmesan and beginning and ending with a layer of rice.
4. Pour sour cream over the top and cook in a 425-degree oven for half an hour, allowing to brown on top.

Makes 3 to 4 servings.

STEWED CHICKEN WITH CRANBERRIES

1 chicken (2½ to 3 pounds)
3 cups buttermilk
Salt and pepper
2 tablespoons butter
2 tablespoons chopped fresh parsley
2 tablespoons chopped fresh mint
1 medium onion, peeled and cut in half
1½ cups chicken broth
1 tablespoon caraway seeds
4 to 6 tablespoons cranberry or lingonberry sauce.

1. Soak the chicken (left whole) in the buttermilk for two hours. Then rinse and wipe the bird dry, salting it inside and out lightly.
2. Brown chicken in hot butter on all sides in deep-sided pot.
3. Place parsley, mint and onion inside the chicken's cavity. Sprinkle bird with caraway seeds and pepper, add broth and stew under cover until it is soft.
4. Divide chicken into serving portions, and move to serving platter, placing a tablespoon of cranberry sauce on each. Pour sauce over chicken and place in a warm oven for 10 minutes.

Makes 4 to 5 servings.

 ## DUCK FRICASSEE WITH MUSHROOM SAUCE

1 duckling (4 to 5 pounds)
Light chicken broth (about 3 cups)
1 bay leaf
½ cup finely chopped onions
Salt and pepper

Mushroom Sauce:

5 tablespoons dried mushrooms
½ cup finely chopped onion
6 tablespoons butter
¼ cup flour
Salt and pepper
¾ cup sour cream
Chopped parsley, for garnish

1. Place the duckling in a pot and add broth to cover. Add the bay leaf, onions, and salt and pepper to taste, and

cook until the duck is tender and easy to take off the bone. Remove duck from the broth and cool before boning.

2. Bone the duck after it has cooled and set the meat aside until the sauce is ready.

For the sauce:

1. Soak the mushrooms in ½ cup boiling water until they are soft. Drain, reserving the liquid. Cut the mushrooms into strips.
2. Sauté the onion in 2 tablespoons of the butter and add to the mushrooms and their liquid. Simmer the two together for a few minutes.
3. Brown the remaining butter in a pan and add the flour. Slowly add the strained and de-fatted broth (the fat may be removed from the broth by skimming the surface or running the broth through a special container which keeps the fat separate) from the duck and the mushroom-onion mixture until it becomes a smooth sauce. Add salt and pepper to taste.
4. Add the sour cream to the sauce and blend well.
5. Place the duck back into the sauce, heat through, and garnish with chopped parsley before serving.

Makes 3 to 4 servings.

LITHUANIAN ROASTED HARE WITH SOUR CREAM

Marinade (recipe follows)
Saddle and thighs of hare (3 to 4 pounds)
¼ pound bacon for larding
Salt and pepper
4 tablespoons butter or lard
3 tablespoons flour
1 cup sour cream
2 tablespoons caramelized sugar

Marinade:

2 cups water
1 cup wine vinegar
½ cup sliced onions
1 bay leaf
3 juniper berries
3 peppercorns

1. Bring the water to a boil and then add all the other marinade ingredients together. Cool.
2. Pour the marinade over the hare and put in a cool place for 3 or 4 days. Turn the pieces of hare every day.
3. Remove from the marinade and dry well.

Preheat oven to 425 degrees.

1. Lard the hare with bacon pieces and season with salt and pepper to taste.
2. Melt the butter in the baking pan, place the hare pieces in it and baste before putting in a 425-degree oven. Add a little water occasionally if the hare becomes dry.
3. Bake for about 2 hours. At the end of the cooking time, remove the hare, cut into serving pieces and keep warm.
4. Add the flour to the baking juices in the pan, a little water if necessary, and the cream. Add the caramelized sugar for color.

The caramelized sugar is made by melting the sugar in a pan until it becomes golden or even light brown in color. An equivalent amount of water is then added and stirred until the mixture becomes a syrup.

Pour the sauce over the meat.

Beets are the perfect vegetable to accompany hare.

Makes 5 to 6 servings.

 ## BRAISED WILD DUCK

1 wild duck (2½ to 3 pounds)
Salt
3 tablespoons butter
6 peppercorns
½ teaspoon marjoram
2 medium onions, sliced
5 dried mushrooms, soaked to soften (liquid for braising)
1 cup broth
1 cup sour cream

Preheat oven to 350 degrees.

1. Cut the duck into serving pieces, rub with salt, and brown in butter.
2. Place duck pieces into a roasting dish, adding the peppercorns, marjoram, onions and dried mushrooms. Add 1 cup broth, the reserved mushroom liquid, and the sour cream.
3. Cover and braise in a 350-degree oven for about 1½ hours.
4. Remove the peppercorns from the sauce before serving.

Makes 3 to 4 servings.

STUFFED PARTRIDGES

3 partridges (1 pound each)
Salt
½ pound chopped veal
1 medium onion, grated
4 tablespoons butter, for brushing and basting
1 tablespoon bread crumbs
Pepper
2 egg yolks
1 cup broth
1 tablespoon flour

Preheat oven to 375 degrees.

1. Rub partridges with salt inside and out, and stuff with the following mixture: chopped veal, onion sautéed in butter, bread crumbs, and salt and pepper to taste. Sew or skewer the birds after stuffing. Brush outside with butter.
2. Place birds in an uncovered roasting pan and bake until they are brown (about 30 minutes).
3. After they are browned, add one cup of hot broth, cover, and braise for about another 30 minutes.
4. Cut the partridges in half lengthwise. Strain the pan juices, add the flour and bring to a boil.
5. Pour the gravy over the birds.

Makes 4 to 5 servings.

YOUNG CHICKEN IN ASPIC

1 small frying chicken (2 pounds), or two Rock Cornish
    hens
6 peppercorns
2 bay leaves
4 cups light chicken or vegetable broth
Salt
1 medium carrot
1 envelope gelatin
Parsley leaves for garnish

1. Cut chicken into four parts, add peppercorns and bay
   leaves, and cook in broth until chicken is soft and can
   easily be removed from its bones. Add salt during the
   last part of cooking.
2. Remove bones from the chicken, cut into smaller sections, and arrange in a shallow dish.
3. Boil the broth to reduce quantity. When it is down to
   about 2 cups, skim off the fat and strain.
4. Add gelatin dissolved in a little cold water and heat the
   broth until gelatin melts.
5. Pour broth over the chicken pieces and decorate with
   pieces of carrot and parsley leaves.

Makes 4 to 5 servings.

ROAST DUCK STUFFED WITH PRUNES AND HAZELNUTS

1 cup chopped pitted prunes
1 cup dry red wine
2 fine slices bacon
1 small onion, chopped
2 cloves garlic, crushed
2 white rolls
¼ cup milk
½ cup peeled hazelnuts
2 tablespoons fresh chopped parsley
1 tablespoon marjoram
Salt and pepper
1 egg
1 large duck (about 6 pounds)

1. Put the chopped prunes into the red wine to soak for 30 minutes.
2. Fry the sliced bacon in a frying pan on medium-high heat until almost crisp. Add the chopped onion and crushed garlic, reduce the heat to medium-low, and fry for another 5 minutes or until the onion is almost golden. Remove from heat and cool.
3. Break up the rolls into small pieces, place in a medium sized bowl and pour on the milk. Let the bread soak up the milk for a few minutes. Then mix in the bacon, garlic and onion mixture. Remove the prunes from the wine and add them, reserving wine for later.
4. Clean the hazelnuts of all skin, chop them roughly and mix into the stuffing. Season with parsley, marjoram, and salt and pepper to taste.
5. Break the egg into the stuffing and mix it in well. If stuffing is still too loose, add another egg to bind it better.

Preheat oven to 400 degrees.

6. Wash the duck and trim off any excess fat. Dry it with paper towels, massage breast gently and prick with a fork to let fat escape during roasting. Season the bird inside and out with salt and pepper.
7. Fill the cavity with stuffing, placing any excess in a separate dish to bake along with the duck. Close the cavity with skewers or string. Place on rack in roasting pan. Pour reserved wine over the duck and place in the oven.
8. After 15 minutes, baste the bird and reduce the heat to 350 degrees. Continue basting occasionally until the duck is tender and its legs move freely (about 2 hours).

Makes 4 servings.

 ## HARE HUNTER STYLE

2 hares (4 to 5 pounds each), marinated for 2 days
    (marinade recipe follows)
6 ounces sliced salt pork or bacon
Bread crumbs for lining
10 to 12 shallots or small white onions, chopped
2 teaspoons paprika
2 cups red wine
Salt and pepper
Dash juniper and thyme

1. Marinate hare for 2 days in marinade recipe below.
2. Line heavy casserole dish with slices of pork or bacon, sprinkle with bread crumbs, then with a layer of chopped shallots. Add paprika.
3. Arrange meat over this and cover with more chopped onion, bacon slices and red wine. Season with salt and pepper to taste, adding juniper and thyme last.
4. Cover tightly and bake in 450-degree oven for 3 hours.

Serve with red cabbage.

Makes 8 to 10 servings.

Marinade for hare and other game:

1 large onion, sliced
1 bay leaf
1 large carrot, sliced
½ celery root, sliced
½ parsley root, sliced
20 peppercorns
10 whole allspice
Dash of thyme
2 to 3 cups wine vinegar
6 cups water

Combine all ingredients and boil for 30 minutes. Cool marinade before meat is immersed. There should be enough marinade to cover meat. Marinate in refrigerator or other cool place, turning occasionally.

FISH

CARP IN GRAY SAUCE

2 cups soup greens (onions, celery and carrot), cubed
1 cup (10) whole peppercorns
4 dried mushrooms
2 to 3 curls of lemon peel
1 slice day-old black bread
2½ to 3 pounds carp, cleaned and left whole

1. Put soup greens, peppercorns, mushrooms and lemon peel, along with bread, into cold water; bring to a boil and simmer for a few minutes.
2. Place carp into boiling broth and cook over low heat for 30 minutes.

Ingredients for sauce:

1 tablespoon flour
1 tablespoon butter
1 lemon, divided
½ cup raisins
1 teaspoon sugar
½ cup almonds (cut in strips)
1 teaspoon white wine

1. Sauté flour in butter, stir in a bit of broth from carp recipe as necessary to achieve paste consistency.
2. Add juice of ½ lemon, raisins, and sugar and heat. Sauce should be sweet and sour.
3. Add almonds and wine.
4. Pour a little sauce over fish, and serve the rest on the side.
5. Garnish the carp with the rest of the lemon, cut into thin slices.

Makes 5 to 6 servings.

PERCH À LA RADZIWILL

1 large or 2 smaller perch (3½ to 4 pounds altogether)
Salt and pepper
1 cup white wine
2 tablespoons melted butter
Buttered white bread, toasted (as many as there are
     pieces of fish)

1. Fillet the fish and cut into square pieces. (Reserve head, bones and skin.) Season with salt and pepper. Arrange in saucepan, add wine and melted butter, and cover with a sheet of greased parchment paper.
2. Cover tightly and steam over low heat for 10 minutes, taking care fillets do not fall apart.
3. Prepare as many pieces of toast as there are serving pieces of fish, making the toast out of buttered bread and using the oven rather than a toaster. Keep hot.

For sauce:

3 cups water
1 large onion, diced
2 to 3 carrots, diced
½ celery root
2 to 3 celery stalks with leaves
1 parsley root
6 peppercorns
1 bay leaf
6 fresh mushrooms, sliced
2 truffles, sliced (optional)
Salt and pepper
½ cup white wine
1 tablespoon butter
1½ teaspoons flour
¼ teaspoon soy sauce
10 crayfish tails or small shrimp, cooked
4 egg yolks, well beaten

1. Cook fish head and bones in the water, with onion, carrots, celery root, celery stalks, parsley root, peppercorns, and bay leaf. Allow liquid to boil down to 2 cups. Strain.
2. Add mushrooms, truffles, salt and pepper to taste, and wine and simmer until mushrooms are done, about 15 to 20 minutes.
3. Blend butter and flour, dissolve with some of the sauce, stirring until smooth, and then combine with other ingredients. Season with soy sauce.
4. Add cooked crayfish or shrimp, and when sauce has bubbled up slowly, stir in the egg yolks, taking care not to let them curdle.
5. Arrange pieces of fish on toast on a large platter, and pour sauce on top.

Makes 6 servings.

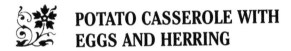

POTATO CASSEROLE WITH EGGS AND HERRING

4 cups peeled, sliced potatoes
1 large or 2 smaller matjes herring
Butter and flour (or bread crumbs) for lining casserole
3 to 4 hard-boiled eggs, sliced
1 tablespoon melted butter
¼ to ½ cup sour cream

Preheat oven to 450 degrees.

1. Parboil potatoes for about 10 minutes and drain.
2. Rinse, bone and chop herring and combine with potatoes.
3. Butter a heavy casserole, dust with flour or bread crumbs and arrange potatoes and sliced eggs in layers, beginning and ending with a layer of potatoes.

4. Add the melted butter and sour cream, season lightly with salt and pepper, and bake covered in a hot oven (450 degrees) for 30 minutes.

This is an excellent Lenten dish.

Makes 4 to 5 servings.

 ## ROAST CARP WITH SOUR CREAM

4 carp fillets
Salt and pepper
1 tablespoon butter
4 shallots, finely sliced
2 tablespoons fresh chopped dill
½ cup sour cream
2 lemons (juice from 1 lemon, and another lemon cut in wedges for garnish)

Preheat oven to 450 degrees.

1. Wash the carp fillets gently in cold water, then dry with paper towels. Season with salt and pepper to taste.
2. Place the fillets in a buttered baking dish, sprinkle with sliced shallots and chopped dill, and cover each fillet with sour cream. Pour on the juice of one lemon.
3. Bake the fish in the oven for about 10 minutes.

Serve with lemon wedges.

Makes 4 servings.

CARP POACHED WITH CARAWAY

4 carp fillets
Salt and pepper
1 tablespoon crushed caraway seeds
1 small onion, finely sliced
2 tablespoons fresh chopped chives, divided
4 tablespoons butter, divided
2 lemons (one juiced and one cut in wedges for garnish)
1 cup dry white wine

1. Wash the carp fillets gently in cold water and dry with paper towels. Season to taste with salt and pepper and add caraway seeds.
2. Place fillets on a large frying pan, add the chopped onion and 1 tablespoon of the chives.
3. Dot with two tablespoons of the butter and pour on the juice of 1 lemon and the white wine. Bring slowly to a boil, reduce the heat, and simmer, uncovered, until done, about 10 minutes.
4. Remove the fish to a serving platter and keep warm in the oven (set on "warm").
5. Raise the heat under the poaching liquid and gradually reduce it by half. Whisk in the remaining butter and adjust the seasonings.
6. Pour the sauce over the fish, and sprinkle on the remaining chives.

Garnish with lemon wedges.

Makes 4 servings.

 **CARP STEWED IN BEER**

2 pounds carp, cleaned and cut into portions
Salt and pepper
1 cup wine vinegar
1½ cups beer
1 tablespoon butter
1 cup bread crumbs
Grated zest of 1 lemon
3 cloves
6 whole peppercorns
1 tablespoon raisins (substitute: 1 tablespoon chopped
    dried apples)

1. Sprinkle carp portions with salt and pepper to taste
   and pour over cold vinegar. Leave it in a cool place for
   30 minutes.
2. Heat the beer and butter in a pot. When the butter is
   melted, add fish portions along with the vinegar it had
   soaked in. Add bread crumbs. Stew for 30 to 40 minutes
   covered.
3. Add the grated lemon zest, and the raisins (or apples) for
   the last few minutes of cooking.

Serve carp with strained sauce poured over it.

Makes 4 servings.

 **PIKE ROULADE**

1 pike, 2½ pounds, cleaned and split lengthwise
Salt and pepper
3 eggs (2 of them separated)
1 slice white bread
½ cup milk for soaking
2 medium onions, chopped fine
1 tablespoon butter
3 cups light broth for aspic
1 envelope gelatin

1. Remove the bones and spread pike out on a cutting board. Sprinkle with salt and pepper and let stand for 30 minutes.
2. For stuffing, beat one egg and two egg yolks with a little milk. Add milk-soaked bread forced through a sieve or food mill, chopped onions, and additional salt and pepper to taste.
3. Sauté this mixture in butter, stirring constantly, until it thickens.
4. Fry the remaining two egg whites separately, cut into small pieces and add to the stuffing.
5. Spread the stuffing on the prepared fish, roll up and wrap in cheese cloth.
6. Boil fish in light broth until it is soft (about 30 minutes). Let fish cool in the broth, then remove the cheese cloth and cut into slices.
7. Place fish slices into a glass dish and cover with strained broth to which gelatin has been added.

Fish may be decorated with vegetables cut into flower shapes before the gelatin is fully set.

Makes 4 to 5 servings.

FISH BALLS IN ASPIC

2 pounds any firm fish, boned
4 tablespoons bread crumbs
1 medium onion, chopped
1 tablespoon olive oil
1 tablespoon butter
1 egg
Salt and pepper
3 cups light broth
1 envelope gelatin

1. Grind the fish in a blender or food processor together with the bread crumbs and the chopped onion (which was first sautéed lightly in olive oil).
2. Add the butter and egg, along with salt and pepper to taste, and form the mixture into small balls. Boil them in the broth. Cool.
3. Strain broth and add gelatin. Pour a little of the aspic mixture into the bottom of a bowl and add the fish balls after the aspic layer becomes firm. Then add the rest of the broth and chill until firm.
4. Unmold onto a platter before serving and decorate with greens and vegetables.

Makes 4 to 5 servings.

FISH CROQUETTES

3 pounds assorted fish, boned and skinned
½ cup bread crumbs
1 medium onion, grated
3 tablespoons butter
2 eggs
½ cup milk
Salt and pepper

1. To make boning easier, but the fish into hot water for a short time. This sets the flesh and makes it easier to remove the bones.
2. Grind the fish together with the bread crumbs, and onion sautéed in some of the butter.
3. Add the eggs, milk, and salt and pepper to taste. Mix well.
4. Form into croquettes, sprinkle with bread crumbs and fry in remaining hot butter.
5. Fry on high heat to start, and lower the heat for the last part of the cooking process.

Makes 8 to 10 servings.

BOILED TROUT WITH SAUCE

1 large or 2 smaller trout (totaling about 3 pounds)
Vegetable broth to cover fish

1. Put the trout in the colander of a fish cooker (or in a regular large pot, wrapped in cheese cloth). Cover with vegetable broth. Simmer, covered, until the broth boils; then lower the heat and cook 30 minutes.
2. When the fish is done, gently remove its skin and keep warm under cover until the sauce is ready.

Sauce for Trout:

1 tablespoon flour
2 tablespoons butter
1 cup light broth
Salt and pepper
1 egg yolk
Juice of ½ lemon

1. Sauté flour in butter until golden, add broth and salt and pepper to taste.
2. Raise the heat and bring to a boil, stirring constantly. Mixture will thicken.
3. Remove from heat, mix in the egg yolk beaten with lemon juice. Mix well and serve immediately.

Makes 5 to 6 servings.

HERRING FRIED IN DOUGH

6 herrings, boned and cleaned
2 eggs, separated
1 tablespoon sour cream
1½ tablespoons flour
5 tablespoons butter for frying

1. Cut herrings in half lengthwise.
2. Beat the egg yolks, add sour cream, flour, and beaten egg
   whites, mixing gently.
3. Dip herring halves in the dough and fry on both sides in
   butter.

Makes 6 servings.

HERRING CROQUETTES WITH RED BEETS

5 herrings, boned and cleaned
2 medium onions, grated
2 tablespoons butter, plus butter for frying
3 medium potatoes, boiled and mashed
2 eggs, plus 1 egg for dipping
4 tablespoons sour cream
Salt and pepper
Bread crumbs for dipping

1. Grind herring in a food processor.
2. Add the onions sautéed in butter, the mashed potatoes,
   eggs, sour cream, and salt and pepper to taste. Mix well
   and shape into croquettes.

3. Dip croquettes in beaten egg, sprinkle with bread crumbs, and fry.

Red Beets:

2 pounds red beets
1 medium onion, chopped
2 tablespoons olive oil
1 tablespoon bread crumbs
½ cup sour cream
Pepper
Vinegar
Salt
Sugar

1. Boil the beets, rinse with cold water so that they may peel more easily, grate and place into a pot.
2. Sauté onion in the olive oil and add to the beets. Add bread crumbs, sour cream, pepper, vinegar, salt, and sugar to taste; mix and heat.
3. Do not overcook, because this tends to make the beets lose their vivid color.

Makes 5 to 6 servings.

HERRING WITH EGGS

2 tablespoons tomato paste
1 teaspoon mustard
Pepper
Sugar
6 herring fillets, cleaned and boned
2 hard-boiled eggs, chopped
Mushrooms for garnish
Vinegar marinade (recipe follows)

1. Mix tomato paste with mustard and chopped eggs. Add pepper and sugar to taste.
2. Mix and spread on the inside of herring pieces. Roll up, put into a dish and pour in vinegar marinade.
3. Keep covered in marinade in a refrigerator overnight. Discard spices used in marinade.
4. Before serving, garnish marinated herring with egg sections and marinated mushrooms.

Makes 6 servings.

Vinegar Marinade:

Salt
Sugar
2 bay leaves
5 cloves
12 peppercorns
1 medium onion, sliced
1 medium carrot, sliced
1 tablespoon chopped parsley
1 stalk celery, chopped
2 cups boiling water
2 cups wine vinegar

1. Place the salt, sugar, bay leaves, cloves, peppercorns, onion, carrot, parsley, and celery into boiling water.
2. Cover the pot, and let simmer over low heat for 20 to 25 minutes.
3. Add the vinegar, return to a boil, and remove from heat immediately. Pour over herring.

This marinade may also be used for preparing the herring in the recipe which follows:

 ## HERRING WITH HORSERADISH SAUCE

6 herrings, cleaned and boned, cut into fillets, and mari-
    nated as in the preceding recipe
Flour for dredging herring, plus 1 tablespoon for sauce
1 cup olive oil, for frying herring and preparing sauce
Horseradish sauce (recipe follows)

1. Roll up marinated herrings, flour, and sauté in olive oil.
2. Arrange on individual plates (usually small, oblong, narrow plates) and pour horseradish sauce on each.

Makes 6 servings.

Horseradish Sauce:

1 tablespoon flour
1 tablespoon olive oil
1 cup horseradish, either prepared or fresh, grated
1 cup sour cream
Vinegar
Sugar
Salt

1. Sauté flour in olive oil, add horseradish and braise.
2. Stir in the sour cream, and heat. Add a few drops of vinegar, sugar, and salt to taste. Mix.
3. Pour over prepared herring.

PANCAKES, NOODLES, DUMPLINGS, & EGG DISHES

PANCAKES

 ## LAYER HAM PANCAKES

Pancake Batter:

2 cups flour
1 teaspoon salt
4 eggs, separated
3 cups milk
Butter for frying

(makes 20 to 24 8-inch pancakes)

1. Combine flour, salt, egg yolks, and 1 cup of the milk, stir-ring until smooth. Gradually stir in the rest of the milk to make a batter the consistency of heavy sweet cream.
2. Beat the egg whites until they are stiff, but not dry, and fold them into the batter. Stir until smooth.
3. Put a little butter with each pancake on a heated 8-inch frying pan and then add about 1½ tablespoons of batter to the pan, tipping it to spread the batter to the edges.
4. Turn to brown both sides of the pancake and pile ready pancakes on top of each other.

Ham Filling:

1 pound chopped boiled ham
2 egg yolks
1 cup sour cream

1. Combine the ham, egg yolks, and cream.
2. Place a freshly baked pancake on a buttered baking dish, spread with 1 tablespoon of filling and repeat until you have used all the pancakes. Only the top pancake should be buttered.

160

3. Place in 350-degree oven until filling is set, about 20 minutes.
4. Cut in pie-fashion and serve hot.

*Another variation of this recipe is to add cooked asparagus to the ham mixture.

Makes 8 to 10 servings.

 ## MEAT-FILLED NALIESNIKAI

3 eggs, separated
Salt
3 cups milk
2 cups flour
Butter for frying

1. Beat the egg yolks with a little salt. Alternating, add milk and flour, a little at a time, to the yolks, and mix well. At first, the dough should be thick so that the flour is mixed in thoroughly; only then should milk be added to make the dough thin.
2. Fold in beaten egg whites.
3. Pour 1 large spoonful into a heated 8-inch pan at a time, just enough to cover the bottom. Cook pancakes on one side only.

Makes 20 to 24 pancakes.

Filling:

1 pound leftover cooked meat (beef, veal, or lamb)
1 medium onion, chopped
Salt and pepper
1 egg
1 cup beef broth

1. Grind meat with onion and salt and pepper in food processor.
2. Add egg and broth and mix well.
3. Spread each pancake (on cooked side) with the mixture; fold edges, roll up, and cut in half.

For final preparation:

2 to 3 eggs, beaten
4 tablespoons bread crumbs
4 tablespoons butter
Parsley or dill

1. Brush each pancake with beaten egg, roll in bread crumbs and sauté in butter until golden.
2. Garnish with parsley or dill if desired.

Makes 8 to 10 servings.

APPLE PANCAKES

4 eggs, separated
1 cup flour
1 tablespoon sour cream
1 cup milk
¼ teaspoon salt
Sugar
2 medium tart apples, grated
Butter for frying

1. Beat the egg yolks until they become light and creamy.
2. Stir in the flour, add the cream, milk, salt and sugar.
3. Add grated apples.
4. Fold in stiffly beaten egg whites.
5. Fry in butter, using 1 large tablespoon of batter per pancake.

Serve with honey or preserves.

Makes 18 to 20 pancakes.

SPECIAL LITHUANIAN PANCAKE

4 tablespoons (½ stick) butter
½ cup flour
½ cup milk
2 eggs
Dash of nutmeg
Salt
1 tablespoon confectioners' sugar
Juice of ½ lemon
Preserves or marmalade

Preheat oven to 450 degrees.

1. Melt the butter and pour into a pie plate.
2. Mix the flour, milk, eggs, nutmeg, and salt. Do not over-beat.
3. Pour into pie plate and bake at 450 degrees for 15 to 20 minutes. Sprinkle with confectioners' sugar and lemon juice.

Serve with marmalade or preserves.

Makes 1 or 2 servings.

NOODLES

 ## NOODLES WITH POPPY SEEDS

Home made noodles (recipe follows), or 8-ounce package
of broad noodles
½ cup poppy seeds
3 to 4 tablespoons sugar
Dash of salt
Melted butter, to pour over noodles before serving

1. Mash poppy seeds with sugar.
2. Prepare noodles, drain and mix with poppy seeds. Season
   with salt and top with melted butter and serve at once.

Noodles:

2 eggs, lightly beaten
½ teaspoon salt
2¼ cups flour
2 to 3 tablespoons water

Add eggs and salt to flour and work on a pastry board,
adding a little lukewarm water to make elastic dough. Add
more flour if necessary. Work until little bubbles begin to
form in dough. Divide in two, roll out very thin on floured
board, and sprinkle with a little flour to help dry. Let stand
a few minutes, then roll up as for jelly roll and cut into
strips. Cook in salted boiling water 5 to 10 minutes,
according to thickness. Makes about 8 ounces.

Makes 5 to 6 servings.

STEAMED NOODLES FOR SOUP

½ cup clarified butter
1 cup flour
4 eggs
1 tablespoon fresh chopped dill
Salt
1 cup water

1. Place the butter into a pan, and add rapidly boiling water.
2. As the butter and water continue boiling, add the flour all at once, and stir until the mixture comes away from the sides of the pan. Remove from the heat and let cool slightly.
3. Add the eggs, one at a time, until the dough becomes fluffy.
4. Add the dill and place bits of the dough by the spoonful into boiling, salted water. When they float to the top, they are ready.
5. Place these noodles into each soup plate before serving.

Makes 5 to 6 servings.

DUMPLINGS

 ## POURED DUMPLINGS

5 eggs, divided
1 tablespoon flour
Salt
4 cups light bouillon

1. Beat the egg whites until stiff and slowly add to them the flour, the egg yolks (one at a time), and a bit of salt to taste.
2. Pour this mixture, one tablespoon at a time, into boiling bouillon; cover and let cook for 4 to 6 minutes, until they all float to the surface.
3. With a large slotted spoon, turn them over in the broth and continue cooking a few minutes longer under cover.
4. Remove from the bouillon and serve immediately with meat or fish.

Makes 4 to 5 servings.

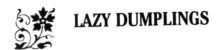

LAZY DUMPLINGS

1 tablespoon butter
4 eggs, separated
1 pound dry pot cheese
2 tablespoons flour
Salt
Bread crumb sauce (recipe follows)

1. Cream butter and egg yolks. Press cheese through sieve.
2. Combine the butter and egg mixture, and the cheese with flour and salt to taste. Mix thoroughly.
3. Fold in stiffly-beaten egg whites.
4. Divide the mixture into two parts and roll each half out on a floured board into a long, thin stick. Flatten and cut on the bias into pieces about 2 inches long.
5. Boil in salted water for 10 to 15 minutes, take out with a perforated spoon, and drain carefully.
6. Serve garnished with bread crumb sauce, which is made as follows:

   3 tablespoons butter and 2 tablespoons bread crumbs. Melt butter and brown lightly. Add bread crumbs and cook over medium heat for another 2 to 3 minutes, just long enough to let the crumbs brown to the color of toast.

Makes 6 servings.

EGG DISHES

 ## BROWNED EGGS

6 poached eggs (recipe follows)
1 egg, beaten (for dipping)
3 tablespoons butter
2 tablespoons bread crumbs

1. Drain poached eggs, dip each one in beaten egg, and sprinkle with bread crumbs.
2. Fry in hot butter on both sides until golden.
3. Arrange on a platter and baste with hot butter before serving.
4. Serve with onion sauce, if desired. Recipe follows.

Makes 6 servings.

Poached eggs:

These are eggs cooked without the shell: the egg white hardens, while the yolk remains soft.

1. Put 1 teaspoon of salt and 2 tablespoons white vinegar into 8 cups of water, and bring to a boil.
2. Break the egg shell and make a clock-wise swirl in the boiling water. Quickly slip the egg into the boiling water. The tartness of the water will rapidly contract the egg white and the egg yolk will remain within the egg white. As soon as the egg white is contracted, remove the eggs with a perforated spoon and place into another pot containing warm water with nothing added to it. This water will remove any tartness that the egg may contain from the previous cooking.

3. The eggs may be kept in the warm water until they are served, at which time they should be placed on paper towels to dry. You may wish to remove any jagged edges of egg white with scissors.

Onion Sauce:

1 tablespoon flour
2 tablespoons butter (divided in two)
2½ cups beef broth
1 large onion, minced
2 tablespoons tomato paste
1 small carrot, grated
1 bay leaf
1 tablespoon wine vinegar
Pepper
Salt
1 teaspoon sugar

1. Sauté flour in 1 tablespoon of the butter. While stirring, slowly dilute with broth and simmer.
2. Add onion, tomato paste, carrot, bay leaf, vinegar, and pepper and simmer for ½ hour. Strain the sauce and add salt and sugar.
3. Just before serving, bring to a boil again and add the remaining butter.

STUFFED EGGS

6 eggs, hard-boiled
Salt and pepper
1 tablespoon sour cream
4 tablespoons finely chopped chives or scallions
2 tablespoons chopped fresh dill
1½ tablespoons bread crumbs
4 tablespoons butter for frying

1. Using a very sharp serrated knife, cut unpeeled eggs lengthwise.
2. Carefully remove the egg yolks and egg whites from the shells, keeping the egg shells unbroken.
3. Chop the egg whites and yolks, and add salt and pepper to taste. Add the sour cream, chives and dill. Mix well and fill the egg shells with this mixture.
4. Sprinkle with bread crumbs. Heat butter in a frying pan, but in the egg halves (shell side up) and sauté.
5. When they are a deep golden color, wipe the shells with a clean cloth and serve.

After they have been sautéed and cooled, these eggs may also be served as appetizers.

Makes 4 to 6 servings.

EGG TOADSTOOLS
(Musmiriai)

6 hard-boiled eggs
¼ cup mayonnaise
1 teaspoon vinegar
1 teaspoon mustard
Salt and pepper
1 bunch parsley
6 tomatoes
1 hard-boiled egg white, chopped fine

1. Peel the hard-boiled eggs. Slice off enough of the heavy end of each egg to permit removal of the yolk, and to allow the eggs to stand upright.
2. Prepare the yolks as for deviled eggs (mixing them with the mayonnaise, vinegar, mustard, and salt and pepper) and stuff the egg whites with this mixture.
3. Stand the eggs upright on a bed of parsley. Cap each egg with a slice of tomato cut from the smooth round side, slightly scooped out.
4. Dot the tomato sparsely with very finely chopped egg-white to resemble toad-stool markings.

CAKES & DESSERTS

EASTER GYPSY CAKE
(Cygan)

12 eggs, separated
4½ to 5 pounds candied orange peel,
    prunes, apricots, figs, dates, raisins (chopped)
¾ cup walnuts, pecans, hazelnuts, roughly chopped
1½ cups sugar
1½ cups flour (Wondra is easiest to blend)
Wafers to line cookie sheet (optional)

1. For 4½ to 5 pounds of fruit, use 12 extra-large eggs, separated.
2. Beat yolks with sugar until light and fluffy. Add to fruit.
3. Whip egg whites till stiff, add to egg and fruit mixture.
4. Last, add flour. (Keeping this sequence makes things much easier to put together.)
5. Pour batter onto a cookie sheet, lined with thin wafers or buttered wax paper.
6. Bake in a 325-degree oven for 1 hour or more until golden brown.

This recipe yields 4 to 5 large, flat cakes. Wrapped in foil, they remain fresh for many weeks.

POPPY SEED POUNDCAKE

½ pound (2 sticks) butter
1 cup poppy seeds
1 cup sour cream
½ cup confectioners' sugar
1 teaspoon baking powder
1 teaspoon baking soda
2 cups flour
4 eggs, separated

1. Whip butter until white and fluffy.
2. Add poppy seeds and sour cream and beat well.
3. Mix sugar, baking powder, baking soda, and flour in a separate bowl.
4. Add a couple tablespoons of the flour mixture and one egg yolk at a time to the butter mixture and beat well. When all the ingredients are used up, beat together until light and fluffy.
5. Fold in beaten egg whites and pour into oblong or tube pan.
6. Bake for 1 hour at 350 degrees.

Makes 8 to 10 servings.

CHRISTMAS BREAD
(Kaledu Paragas)

1 yeast cake or 1 package dry yeast
¼ cup butter
¼ cup sugar
1½ teaspoons salt
½ cup scalded milk
¼ cup cold water
3 cups all-purpose flour
1 egg
1½ cups golden raisins
¼ cup honey, warmed slightly
¼ cup poppy seeds

1. Dissolve yeast in ¼ cup lukewarm water.
2. Combine butter, sugar, salt, milk and cold water. Add flour and mix till blended thoroughly. Add the egg and raisins.
3. Grease a pan (9 × 5 × 3) and pour mixture into it.
4. Cover with clean dish towel and let rise in a warm place (85 degrees) for about 1½ hours.
5. Bake in a 350-degree oven for 50 to 60 minutes.
6. Before the last 5 minutes of baking, remove from oven, brush with warmed honey and sprinkle with poppy seeds. Return to oven to finish baking.

Makes 8 to 10 servings.

KAIMAK
(Lithuanian Easter Cake)

4 cups milk
4 cups sugar
2 teaspoons vanilla (or a stick of vanilla, to be removed
    before cooling)
1 tablespoon butter
1 cup walnuts, ground
1 tablespoon grated orange peel
Juice of ½ lemon
Crisp bottom layer (recipe follows)

1. Cook the milk with the sugar and vanilla over medium
   heat, stirring occasionally until it thickens.
2. When the mixture becomes thick, add the butter, walnuts, orange peel and lemon juice and stir well.
3. Pour out over a crisp bottom layer and cool.

Crisp Bottom Layer:

2 cups flour
¼ teaspoon salt
½ teaspoon baking powder
⅔ cup (12 tablespoons) butter
2 egg yolks
2 tablespoons heavy cream
½ teaspoon grated lemon peel

1. Combine the flour, salt and baking powder in a large
   bowl. Cut the butter in with a pastry blender until the
   mixture resembles coarse crumbs.
2. Add the sugar, egg yolks, cream and lemon peel. Toss
   lightly with a fork and knead for 1 or 2 minutes until the
   dough becomes smooth. Refrigerate for 30 minutes.
   Preheat oven to 350 degrees.

3. Lightly grease a medium cookie sheet and place the dough on it (either by rolling with a rolling pin or simply patting down with your hands).
4. Bake until golden in color, about 15 to 20 minutes. Cool before covering with milk mixture.

Makes 8 to 10 servings.

 ## CRANBERRY PUDDING
(Kisiel)

This pudding is often served on Christmas Eve.

2 pounds fresh cranberries, picked over and rinsed
3 cups cold water
Sugar to taste
Potato flour (1 teaspoon for every cup of fruit pulp)
2 teaspoons vanilla

1. Cook cranberries with water for about 20 minutes and cool slightly.
2. Force through sieve or food mill.
3. Measure resulting pulp, reserving ½ cup for dissolving potato flour (along with a bit of cold water) to be added later.
4. Add sugar to taste and boil for 10 minutes.
5. Slowly add reserved cool pulp with potato flour and stir for 2 to 3 minutes to avoid lumps.
6. When mixture is cool, add vanilla and cover with plastic wrap. Refrigerate.

Serve with sweet cream.

Makes 8 to 10 servings.

EASTER CHEESE DESSERT
(Paskha)

2 pounds farmer's cheese
5 egg yolks
¾ pound confectioners' sugar
1 cup heavy cream
¼ pound almonds, coarsely chopped
¼ pound golden raisins
1 cup candied orange peel, cut into small pieces
2 teaspoons vanilla extract
½ pound (2 sticks) unsalted butter, room temperature

1. Strain cheese through sieve or food mill. Set aside.
2. Mix yolks with sugar. Add cream. Heat mixture, just short of bringing to a boil. Take off stove, add cheese, almonds, raisins, orange peel, and vanilla. Add softened and whipped butter. Combine thoroughly.
3. Wrap mixture in cheese cloth, and place in colander or clean flower pot. Weigh down with heavy can and let run off in a cool place for a few days.
4. Mold into pyramid shape with your hands. Decorate with almonds, orange peel, gum drops and green leaves.

Makes 10 to 12 (very rich) servings.

 ## ALMOND TORTE IN SHELL

Pastry:

2 cups flour
1 cup sugar
½ pound (2 sticks) sweet butter
Dash of salt

1. Sift flour, combine with remaining ingredients and work until smooth. Let stand in a cool place 15 to 30 minutes.
2. Roll out thin on floured pastry board.
3. Line a buttered baking tin with the dough, leaving enough dough for covering.

Filling:

4 cups almonds, blanched and peeled
1½ teaspoons vanilla extract
2 cups sugar
6 whole eggs
6 eggs, separated

1. Grind almonds. Add vanilla and sugar, and blend with the whole eggs, adding the eggs one by one.
2. Then add the egg yolks, also one by one, creaming until the mixture becomes light and creamy in color.
3. Add stiffly beaten egg whites.
4. Turn into pastry shell, cover with a thin layer of dough, press edges together and bake in a 375-degree oven for 45 minutes to 1 hour, or until nicely brown.

Ice if desired with transparent icing, which is prepared as follows:

Combine 2 cups confectioners' sugar with enough water, added a little at a time, to make a mixture which may be easily spread with a knife. Work in a bowl with a wooden spoon until transparent. Add a dash of rum for flavoring and spread over cake. Let stand in slightly warm oven for 5 minutes.

POPPY SEED TORTE

⅔ cup sweet butter
⅔ cup sugar
5 egg yolks
1 cup poppy seeds (about ½ pound)
2 tablespoons honey
1 tablespoon flour

1. Cream butter, sugar and egg yolks until light and cream colored.
2. Blanch and drain poppy seeds and then grind them.
3. Combine egg mixture, poppy seeds, honey and flour, and pour into buttered mold well dusted with flour.
4. Bake 30 minutes in 350-degree oven.

May also be baked with the addition of 5 stiffly beaten egg whites for a fluffier consistency.

Makes 4 to 5 servings.

APPLE MAZUR IN SHORT SHELL

Dough:

½ pound (2 sticks) unsalted butter
2 cups almonds, blanched, peeled and ground
1 cup sugar
4 eggs, lightly beaten
2 cups flour

1. Cream butter, combine with ground almonds, sugar, eggs and flour, and work until thoroughly blended.
2. Roll out ¼-inch thick.
3. Bake in greased pan in 350-degree oven until nicely brown, about 15 to 20 minutes.

Topping:

1 cup sugar
¼ cup water
6 to 7 sour apples (like Granny Smith), peeled, cored and sliced thin
Grated lemon or orange rind for flavoring (about 2 teaspoons)

1. Make a thick syrup of sugar and water, and cook for 5 minutes.
2. Add apples and rind and simmer until apples turn transparent and begin to fall apart, stirring to prevent burning. (If too thick, add more water.)
3. When the apple mixture begins to separate from edges of the pan, take off the heat and allow to cool a bit.
4. Spread over the pre-baked layer of cake and allow to cool again.

Makes 6 to 8 servings.

 **SPICE CAKE**

4 cups honey
5 eggs, separated
4 cups flour
1 teaspoon baking powder
1 cup almonds
1 cup citron
2 tablespoons finely chopped orange peel
¼ teaspoon ground cloves
½ teaspoon cinnamon
dash of nutmeg

1. Heat honey, skim, and simmer until it darkens. Pour into a bowl and work with wooden spoon.
2. When cool, add the egg yolks one at a time and continue creaming.
3. Sift in flour and baking soda and mix thoroughly.
4. Add almonds, citron, orange peel, cloves, cinnamon and nutmeg (increasing amount of spices if a more spicy taste is preferred).
5. Pour into well-greased mold dusted with flour and bake in low-temperature oven (325 degrees) for one hour.

Best when allowed to stand 10 to 14 days before using.

Makes 8 to 10 servings.

POPPY SEED PUFF

1 cup poppy seeds
6 eggs, separated
½ cup sugar
½ cup almonds, blanched and chopped fine
4 tablespoons bread crumbs
Butter and bread crumbs for lining baking dish

1. Blanch and drain poppy seeds, then grind.
2. Cream egg yolks and sugar until cream-colored and combine with poppy seeds.
3. Add almonds and bread crumbs and mix thoroughly.
4. Fold in stiffly beaten egg whites.
5. Pour into buttered pastry form lined with bread crumbs.
6. Bake in 350-degree oven for 30 minutes.

Serve with the following white wine sauce:

5 egg yolks
5 tablespoons sugar
2 cups white wine

1. Beat sugar and egg yolks until very light.
2. Place over boiling water in a double boiler and slowly add the wine, beating constantly with a rotary beater.
3. The sauce is ready when it is thick and foamy. Care must be taken not to overcook and curdle.

If sauce is to be served hot, prepare directly before serving; otherwise, chill in refrigerator.

Makes 6 servings.

KINDLING OR FAVORS
(Two variations)

Variation I.

2 cups flour
1 tablespoon butter, melted
2 heaping tablespoons sugar
1 egg, lightly beaten
1 tablespoon white vinegar
½ cup sour cream (approximately)
Shortening for frying
confectioners' sugar for sprinkling

1. Combine flour with butter, sugar and egg and stir ingredients together.
2. Add vinegar and sour cream to form dough the consistency of biscuit dough—just solid enough to roll. Divide into four parts.
3. Roll one piece very thin on floured board, keeping the rest covered to prevent drying.
4. Cut into strips about 1 inch wide and 5 inches long. Cut a short lengthwise slit in the center of each strip and pass one end of the strip through the slit. Repeat until all of the dough is used up.
5. Fry in shortening (such as Crisco) until golden brown, drain on paper and sprinkle with confectioners' sugar.

NOTE: A piece of raw potato should be placed into the hot fat to prevent pastry from burning.

Variation II.

6 egg yolks
6 tablespoons sugar
1 cup sweet cream
2 tablespoons rum
2 cups flour (approximately)

1. Beat egg yolks with sugar until creamy white. Combine with cream and rum; then add enough flour so that dough can be rolled out very thin.
2. Divide into four parts, then proceed with steps 3 to 5 in variation number I.

Makes a large platter of cookies.

 ## APPLE CHARLOTTE

10 large tart apples (such as Granny Smith)
Sugar
Cinnamon to taste (optional)
1 tablespoon butter
2 tablespoons apricot jam
2 tablespoons seedless raisins
Slices of white bread

1. Core and pare apples and slice them thin.
2. Combine apples, sugar and cinnamon (if used) to taste, and butter. Simmer, tightly covered, for about 10 minutes.
3. Add jam and raisins and mix thoroughly.
4. Remove crusts from bread, cut in half and toast.
5. Line buttered baking dish with slightly overlapping slices of toast, pour in apple mixture, cover top with more toast and bake in hot oven (425 degrees) for 30 to 40 minutes.

May be served with whipped cream.

Makes 6 to 7 servings.

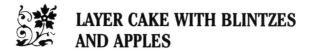 **LAYER CAKE WITH BLINTZES AND APPLES**

½ cup sugar
2 sticks (½ pound) butter, divided
1 cup cream
4 eggs, separated
1 tablespoon grated lemon peel
1 cup flour
½ pound tart apples, peeled and finely cut
1 tablespoon powdered sugar
1 tablespoon vanilla
3 tablespoons sugar to add to egg whites

1. Cream sugar with 1 stick butter. Add cream, egg yolks and mix well. Combine with grated lemon peel.
2. Gradually add flour and knead dough well.
3. Fry thin blintzes in ½ stick hot butter. Cover with towel to keep warm.
4. Place finely cut apples in pan, sprinkle with powdered sugar and vanilla, add ½ stick of butter and stew for 10 to 15 minutes until they become soft.
5. Place 1 tablespoon stewed apples in the middle of each blintz, roll them up and place in a greased baking dish in two layers, one on top of the other.
6. Cover with egg whites whipped with sugar and bake in a 350-degree oven for 15 to 20 minutes.

Makes 6 to 8 servings.

STRAWBERRIES IN CUSTARD SAUCE

2 pounds strawberries
½ cup sugar, divided
1 teaspoon potato starch or cornstarch
3 eggs, divided
1 teaspoon vanilla
1½ cups milk, heated

1. Mix strawberries, stems removed, with ¼ cup sugar. Set aside.
2. Dissolve starch in a little warm water. Mix egg yolks with starch, remaining sugar and vanilla, then add whipped egg whites.
3. Put in double boiler. Stir the mixture while water is simmering, gradually adding hot milk until sauce thickens.
4. Set pot of thickened sauce over cold water or ice and continue whipping until totally chilled.

Serve strawberries with prepared sauce.

Makes 5 to 6 servings.

APPLES WITH CHEESE STUFFING

1 pound tart apples
⅓ pound farmer's cheese
1 egg
1½ tablespoons sugar
¾ cup fruit or berry syrup (black currant syrup works
    well here)

1. Wash and peel apples. Cut them in half and remove core.
2. Stuff prepared apples with grated farmer cheese mixed
   with raw egg and sugar. Place in casserole sprinkled with
   water to prevent burning.
3. Bake in 325-degree oven for 10 to 15 minutes or until
   tender.

Serve warm with fruit or berry syrup.

Makes 4 to 5 servings.

MERINGUE APPLES

8 sweet dessert apples
4 egg whites
⅔ cup confectioners' sugar
A pinch of cinnamon (optional)

Preheat oven to 350 degrees.

1. Peel apples and remove core. Place in pot with boiling water and bring back to a boil. Remove and dry apples.
2. Place apples in a buttered over-proof dish.
3. Whip the egg whites until stiff and add confectioners' sugar and a pinch of cinnamon (optional). Spoon over apples and bake for about 15 minutes.

To make accompanying sauce:

1½ cups sweet cream
4 egg yolks
3 tablespoons sugar
1 teaspoon vanilla

1. Bring cream to a boil.
2. Cream egg yolks with sugar until light in color.
3. Add egg mixture to hot cream carefully, making sure not to make scrambled eggs. When mixture has cooled (can be placed over ice cubes if sauce is needed in a hurry), add vanilla.

Serve with meringue apples.

Makes 8 servings.

COUNTRY GIRL BRAID

2 packets active dry yeast
½ cup warm water
¾ cup lukewarm milk
¼ cup sugar
1 teaspoon salt
⅓ cup shortening
2 eggs
1 teaspoon grated lemon rind
4½ to 4¾ cups flour
½ cup candied fruit
½ cup raisins
Almonds and cherries for garnish, if desired.

Frosting:

1½ cups confectioners' sugar
Enough water to make a thin and easily
spread consistency
½ teaspoon vanilla or rum for flavoring

1. Soak yeast in warm water for five minutes.
2. Pour lukewarm milk over sugar and salt in a large mixing bowl and stir.
3. Beat in shortening, eggs, grated lemon rind, yeast mixture and one cup of flour until smooth. Stir in fruit and raisins. Add remaining flour, mixing well until the dough leaves the sides of the bowl.
4. Turn out onto a lightly floured board. Knead until dough becomes smooth and elastic, and is no longer sticky (5 to 10 minutes). Place in lightly greased bowl. Grease top of dough and cover with waxed paper or plastic wrap.
5. Let rise in a warm place until it is doubled in bulk, about 1 to 1½ hours. Punch down.
6. Preheat oven to 350 degrees.

7. Divide dough into four equal parts. Shape three parts into strips 14 inches long. Place on a lightly greased baking sheet and form into a braid.
8. Divide the remaining portion into three parts and form strips nine inches long. Then, form these into a smaller braid, place on top of the larger braid, and tuck under all ends.
9. Let rise in a warm place until doubled in bulk, about 45 to 60 minutes. Bake for 40 to 50 minutes. Frost while it is still warm by drizzling sugar frosting across the top of the braid.

Garnish with almonds and cherries if desired.

Makes 8 to 10 servings.

 ## PLUM DUMPLINGS

1 pound fresh prune plums (which appear in the Fall)
3 cups flour
Pinch of salt
½ packet dry yeast
1 teaspoon sugar
¾ cup warm milk, divided
1 egg
Sugar for sprinkling over cooked dumplings
8 tablespoons melted butter
½ cup sour cream (optional)
½ cup farmer cheese (optional)

1. Wash and dry the plums, cut them in half and remove their pits.
2. Mix together the flour and salt in a large bowl. Make a well in the center and put in the yeast and the sugar. Mix together the yeast, sugar and a little of the flour.

3. Slowly add ½ cup of the milk which has been warmed on the stove. Put a warm, damp cloth over the bowl and leave for about 20 minutes or until the yeast mixture has risen a little.

4. Add the remaining ¼ cup of milk into the yeast mixture and begin to stir in the remaining flour. Break the egg into the flour and keep mixing it until you have a thick paste.

5. Turn the dough out onto a floured board or table. Knead it very quickly and lightly just enough to have it form a ball. Then, using a rolling pin, roll it out quite thin (about ⅛ of an inch). Cut the dough into squares with 2-inch sides.

6. Put half a plum in each square, wrap the dough around the plum, and seal the edges by pinching the sides together.

7. Bring a large pot of water to a rapid boil. Put about a dozen of the plums into the boiling water at a time. Once the dumplings have risen to the surface of the water, boil them for another 5 minutes. Put a sieve next to the pot and transfer the cooked dumplings into it, piercing each of them with a fork to release steam.

Serve with sugar, melted butter, farmer cheese, or sour cream.

If the dumplings are served as a dessert, 3 of them per person are ample; 4 or 5 of them can make a light meal.

APPLE FRITTERS

2 large apples
2 teaspoons sugar, divided
4 tablespoons rum or brandy, divided
2 eggs
Pinch of salt
¾ cup flour
¼ cup milk
4 tablespoons butter
Confectioners' sugar or whipped cream for garnish

1. Peel and core the apples, then cut them into thin slices. Place them in a bowl, sprinkle with 1 teaspoon of sugar and pour on 2 tablespoons of the rum or brandy. Mix well and set aside for about 30 minutes.
2. To make batter, break the eggs into a bowl and mix in the remaining sugar and rum or brandy, along with a pinch of salt. Slowly add the flour, mixing well.
3. Add as much of the milk as necessary to form a fairly thick batter. Add the apple slices and mix well.
4. Heat the butter over medium heat in a large frying pan. When the butter bubbles have subsided, make three or four fritters by scooping up some of the apple-batter with a ladle, placing it in the frying pan, and shaping it into a rough circle.
5. Fry the apple fritters until golden brown on each side, about 3 to 4 minutes per side. Repeat until all the fritters are done.

May be served with confectioners' sugar or whipped cream.

Makes 4 to 6 servings.

APPLE STRUDEL

Strudel dough is very time-consuming to make, but fortunately we now have good quality frozen Phyllo dough available.

2 pounds apples
6 tablespoons butter, divided
½ cup sugar
1 teaspoon ground cinnamon
½ cup raisins
Zest of 1 lemon
1 package Phyllo pastry
Flour for dusting board
½ cup fine bread crumbs
½ cup melted butter (separate from 6 tablespoons
    mentioned above)
Confectioners' sugar for dusting
Whipped cream for garnish (optional)

1. To prepare the filling, peel and core the apples, then slice them thin. Put them in a mixing bowl and add 4 tablespoons of the butter, the sugar, cinnamon, raisins, and grated lemon zest. Mix well.
2. To prepare the pastry, put in onto a floured board and roll out very thin (about ⅛ of an inch) into a large rectangle.

Preheat oven to 350 degrees.

3. Melt the remaining 2 tablespoons of butter over medium heat in a small pan and add the bread crumbs. Brown them quickly.
4. Slather the pastry with most, but not all of the melted ½ cup of butter. Sprinkle on the browned bread crumbs.

5. Spread the apple filling all over the pastry. Roll up the strudel and tuck in the ends to make a long loaf.
6. Place the strudel on a buttered baking tin and brush with the remaining melted butter.
7. Put the strudel in the oven and bake for about 30 minutes, or until golden brown. Let cool, then dust with confectioners' sugar.

May be garnished with whipped cream.

Makes 8 servings.

 ## CIDER PUDDING

6 cups apple cider, divided
Sugar
1 stick cinnamon
Peel of 1 lemon
1 cup potato starch

1. Simmer 3 cups of the cider with the sugar, cinnamon and lemon peel for about 15 minutes. Remove and discard the cinnamon stick and lemon peel.
2. Dissolve the potato starch in the remaining 3 cups of cider and add to the boiling cider, stirring vigorously.
3. Mix well, bring to a boil, and pour into a mold which has been rinsed in cold water and sprinkled with sugar.
4. Cool in the refrigerator overnight before unmolding.

Makes 6 servings.

TORTE WITH GELATIN

3 eggs, separated
3 tablespoons sugar
Juice of 1 lemon
1 cup bread crumbs (made from fresh black bread)
Apple juice or apple brandy for sprinkling
4 medium apples, peeled and cut into sections
1 envelope (¼ ounce) gelatin
2 cups apple juice or cider

Preheat oven to 325 degrees.

1. Beat the egg yolks with sugar, add the lemon juice. Add the bread crumbs and mix.
2. Fold in beaten egg whites, and bake for 25 to 30 minutes.
3. After the torte has cooled, sprinkle lightly with apple juice or apple brandy to moisten.
4. Cook the apples in a small amount of water until they are softened but still retain their shape. Arrange the apple pieces over the torte in a circular fashion.
5. Make the gelatin with apple juice instead of water according to package directions (2 cups of liquid to 1 envelope of gelatin), cool to thicken slightly and pour over the torte. Chill before serving.

Other fruit in season may be substituted for the apples.

Makes 4 to 5 servings.

BREAD AND APPLE CASSEROLE

2 cups black bread crumbs (made from fresh bread)
1 cup cranberry juice
6 medium apples, grated
1 cup sugar
Cinnamon
2 tablespoons butter
1 apple, sliced (for garnish)

Preheat oven to 325 degrees.

1. Moisten the bread crumbs with cranberry juice.
2. Mix the grated apples with sugar and cinnamon, to taste.
3. Grease a casserole dish with a little butter, and put in bread and apple mixture in layers. End with a layer of sliced apple on top. Garnish with sliced apple before baking. Dot with remaining butter and bake for about 30 minutes.

Lithuanians sometimes serve this dessert with sweetened milk, which is made in the following manner:

To two cups of fresh milk, add 1 to 2 tablespoons of sugar and a very thin rind of lemon. Let stand for about one hour and strain.

Makes 4 to 5 servings.

APPLES IN MERINGUE

8 medium apples, peeled and cored
6 egg whites
½ cup sugar
Cinnamon

1. Steam the apples in a little water until they are soft but still not mushy.

Preheat oven to 325 degrees.

2. Drain the apples and place them in a greased casserole dish.
3. Beat the egg whites, slowly adding the sugar and cinnamon to taste. Arrange the mixture on top of the apples.
4. Bake for 20 to 25 minutes, until the meringue gains a little color. Serve warm.

ALMOND "BOBA"

12 eggs, divided
1 cup sugar
1¼ cup almonds, ground
1 cup flour
Butter for greasing the pan and bread crumbs for sprinkling

Preheat oven to 375 degrees.

1. Cream egg yolks with sugar until they turn creamy white.
2. Add ground almonds and mix well.
3. Sift in the flour and gently fold in beaten egg whites.
4. Butter baking pan and sprinkle with bread crumbs.
5. Bake for about 1 hour.
6. Let the "boba" cool in the baking pan before removing.

Makes 7 to 8 servings.

COOKED EGG YOLK SQUARE

10 hard-boiled egg yolks
1 cup sugar
Juice of 1 lemon
2 raw eggs
½ cup melted butter
1 cup flour
Wafers to line the bottom of the baking sheet

Preheat oven to 325 degrees.

1. Remove the yolks from the hard-boiled eggs. Cream them with the sugar and lemon juice.
2. Add 2 raw eggs and the melted butter, a little at a time. Add flour and mix.
3. Line a baking sheet with wafers [sheets of unsweetened wafers are often available in larger ethnic (Polish and Hungarian) food stores], add egg mixture, and bake for 20 to 30 minutes.

Makes 6 to 8 servings.

DRIED FRUIT SQUARE

6 eggs, separated
1 cup sugar
½ cup flour
½ cup potato starch
1 cup currants
1 cup mixed dried fruits, cut into small pieces
½ cup roughly chopped walnuts or almonds
1 teaspoon cinnamon-clove mixture (optional)
Thin wafers to line baking sheet

Preheat oven to 325 degrees.

1. Cream the egg yolks with sugar until they become creamy white.
2. Add a mixture of flour and potato starch, a little at a time. Add fruit, nuts, and cinnamon-clove mixture, and mix well.
3. Fold in beaten egg whites.
4. Line baking sheet with wafers (see previous recipe) and bake for 35 to 40 minutes.

Makes 6 to 8 servings.

 FILLED SQUARE

6 cups flour
½ pound (2 sticks) butter
1½ cups sugar
3 eggs
1 teaspoon baking powder
1 teaspoon vanilla
Butter for greasing baking pan
2 cups preserves
Confectioners' sugar for sprinkling

1. Knead all the ingredients (except preserves and confectioners' sugar), mixing them together thoroughly.
2. Cover the dough with a cloth and put in a cool place to set. After a couple of hours, divide the dough in half.

Preheat oven to 425 degrees.

3. Crumble half of the dough into a prepared baking pan, spoon preserves (of your choice) over the crumbs. Crumble the other half of the dough on top of the preserves.

4. Bake for 45 to 50 minutes.
5. After removing from the oven, sprinkle with confectioners' sugar.

Makes 10 to 12 servings.

 ## SQUARE SPREAD WITH PRESERVES

2 tablespoons butter, plus some for buttering the baking pan
3 cups flour
1 teaspoon baking powder
4 egg yolks
1 cup sugar
Grated peel of ½ lemon
2 cups preserves
1 egg, for brushing

Preheat oven to 425 degrees.

1. Cut butter into the flour, which has been mixed with the baking powder.
2. Cream the egg yolks with sugar and lemon peel.
3. Add to flour mixture and knead to mix.
4. Roll out ⅔ of the dough, place in a greased baking sheet and bake until half done (about 30 minutes).
5. Remove from the oven, quickly spread with the preserves, and decorate with strips of the remaining dough, criss-cross fashion. Brush top strips with beaten egg.
6. Place back in the oven for about another 30 minutes.

Makes 6 to 8 servings.

 # FRUIT TART

2 cups flour
8 tablespoons (1 stick) butter
1 egg
½ cup sugar
A few tablespoons of milk, as needed
Butter to grease pan
1 egg to brush on dough
Slices of various seasonal fruits

Preheat oven to 350 degrees.

1. Knead together the flour, butter, egg, sugar, and milk until thoroughly mixed.
2. Roll out a thin layer and spread it over a greased baking dish.
3. Make a braided edge, using a bit of the same dough, and arrange it around the baking dish.
4. Prick dough with a fork, brush with beaten egg and bake until dough becomes slightly golden, about 15 to 20 minutes. Remove from the oven and cool a little before proceeding.

After dough has cooled, arrange fruit slices on top. If several fruits are used, do not mix them, but make a row of each. Cover the tart with the following mixture:

2 eggs, separated
2 tablespoons sugar
2 tablespoons sweet cream
1 tablespoon farina

1. Cream the egg yolks with the sugar until creamy white, add the cream and beat well.

2. Fold in the beaten egg whites, sprinkle with the farina, and mix gently.
3. Pour this mixture over the fruit and bake until the top sets (15 to 25 minutes).

Makes 5 to 6 servings.

 ## LITTLE STICK COOKIES

3 cups flour
1 cup sugar
1 egg yolk
½ pound (2 sticks) butter

1. Knead together the flour, sugar, egg yolk, and butter. Mix well. Let the dough stand in a cool place to set for about one hour.

Preheat oven to 350 degrees.

2. Force the dough through a cookie press to shape into little sticks (if you have one). If not, roll into little sticks by hand and place on an ungreased cookie sheet.
3. Sprinkle each stick with the following mixture:

   2 tablespoons sugar
   ½ cup chopped nuts

4. Bake for about 15 to 20 minutes.

Makes 40 to 50 little cookies.

 **STEP COOKIES**

2½ cups flour
½ cup sugar
½ pound (2 sticks) butter
1 cup nuts (walnuts, hazelnuts, or almonds), ground
1 teaspoon vanilla
1 teaspoon baking powder
1 cup preserves (whatever kind you like) for filling

1. Make dough, using all of the above ingredients except for the preserves. Knead to mix them thoroughly.
2. Put the dough in a cool place to set for about one hour.

Preheat oven to 350 degrees.

3. Roll the dough out to a thickness of ⅛ inch. Using three different sizes of round cookie cutters, cut out equal numbers of each size, place on an ungreased cookie sheet and bake until the cookies turn golden (about 20 minutes). Cool slightly.
4. Spread the centers of the baked cookies with the preserves and put one of each of the three sizes on top of one another. The smallest, top cookie may then be garnished with a berry or half an almond.

Makes 20 to 25 cookies.

 **ALMOND COOKIES**

½ cup ground almonds
14 tablespoons butter (2 tablespoons short of 2 sticks)
2 eggs
1 egg, separated
½ cup sugar, plus 1 tablespoon to sprinkle on top
2 ¾ cups flour

Preheat oven to 350 degrees.

1. Cream the almonds with butter.
2. When this mixture becomes smooth and creamy, add two eggs and one egg yolk, add sugar, and beat until it becomes fluffy.
3. Add flour, and knead the mixture into a dough. Roll out to a thickness of ⅛ inch.
4. Cut out various shapes of cookies and place them on an ungreased cookie sheet.
5. Brush the cookies with the remaining egg white and sprinkle with sugar. Bake until golden, about 20 to 25 minutes.

Makes 30 to 40 cookies, depending on size you choose.

APPLE UPSIDE-DOWN CAKE

1 cup flour
1 cup confectioners' sugar, plus a little for sprinkling
½ teaspoon cinnamon
8 tablespoons butter
6 apples, peeled and cut into small sections
Juice of ½ lemon

Preheat oven to 350 degrees.

1. Sift together the flour, sugar, and cinnamon.
2. Cut the butter into the flour mixture until small crumbs form.
3. Arrange apple sections in a circular pattern on the baking dish. Sprinkle with lemon juice.
4. Cover the apples evenly with the dough crumbs and bake for 35 to 45 minutes.
5. After the cake has cooled, invert it on a platter and sprinkle with powdered sugar.

**In another variation of this cake, the baking dish is placed on the stove with a ½ cup of sugar and a little butter until the sugar becomes brown and caramelized. Then the apples are placed in it as described above. When the dish is inverted after baking, the cake has a nice caramelized look.

Makes 5 to 6 servings.

 **BIRCH LOG**

9 egg yolks
1½ cups sugar
Juice of 1 lemon
Grated rind of 2 lemons
10 egg whites
1¾ cups flour
1 teaspoon baking powder
Butter or shortening for greasing pan

Preheat oven to 350 degrees.

1. Cream the egg yolks and sugar. Add lemon juice and rind.
2. Beat the egg whites until stiff and add to the mixture alternately with the flour and baking powder.
3. Pour into a jelly-roll pan or cookie sheet lined with greased paper. Bake for 15 to 20 minutes.
4. Cut off and reserve one-third of the cake; place the rest on a dish towel, spread with filling (recipe follows) and roll up.
5. Roll the reserved portion of the cake into 3 or 4 smaller rolls ("branches") of unequal thickness. Cut one end of each diagonally, and attach to the large roll ("log") with icing, at different angles. Frost the entire surface with white frosting (recipe follows). Make birch-bark markings with either a fork or with bottled liquid chocolate.

Filling:

3 cups pitted prunes
1 cup sugar
2 sticks butter
2 egg yolks
1 teaspoon vanilla
2 tablespoons cocoa

1. Boil the prunes. Drain and force the pulp through a sieve or food mill.
2. Cream the sugar and butter. Add the egg yolks and beat well.
3. Add the prune pulp to the egg mixture, along with the vanilla and cocoa.

White Frosting:

2 egg whites
1½ cups sugar
¼ teaspoon cream of tartar
⅓ cup cold water
A dash of salt
1 teaspoon vanilla

Boil water in the lower part of a double boiler, and keep over a low flame.

1. Place all ingredients except for vanilla (egg whites, sugar, cream of tartar, water, and salt) into the top part of double boiler and beat until well blended.
2. Put the top of double boiler over the lower part and beat constantly until the frosting forms stiff peaks (this takes about 7 minutes). Remove from heat.
3. Pour into a mixing bowl, add vanilla and beat a further 2 minutes until frosting is of a spreading consistency.

PORCUPINE CAKE
(Eziukai)

10 egg yolks
1½ cups sugar
1½ cups poppy seeds
A bit of flour and potato starch for sprinkling
12 egg whites
1 cup dry white bread crumbs
1 tablespoon melted butter
1½ teaspoons baking powder
½ teaspoon grated lemon rind
½ cup almonds

Preheat oven to 350 degrees.

1. Cream the yolks and sugar. Add parboiled and drained poppy seeds which have been sprinkled with a little flour and potato starch.
2. Add stiffly beaten egg whites. Combine mixture with the bread crumbs, butter, baking powder, and lemon rind.
3. Bake in a greased shallow pan for 20 to 30 minutes.
4. Cut a "foundation" piece in the outline form of a porcupine. Spread with filling (recipe follows), and build up into a rounded porcupine body, using progressively smaller cut pieces of cake, spreading each layer with filling. Shape carefully to resemble a porcupine.
5. Cut a small, round piece of cake for the head, and attach it to the body with a tooth-pick. Use cloves for eyes.
6. Ice entire cake (recipe follows).

For almond quills, use slivered almonds which have been slightly browned in the oven or in a pan.

Filling:

5 eggs
1⅜ cups sugar
1⅜ cups butter
1 teaspoon vanilla or a liqueur you like

1. Beat the eggs on top of a double boiler. While the eggs are heating, gradually stir in the sugar. Heat and stir until the mixture becomes thick.
2. Cream the room-temperature butter. When eggs have cooled a bit, slowly beat in the creamed butter, a little at a time. Add the vanilla or other flavoring.

Icing:

2 cups sugar
½ cup water
1 teaspoon lemon juice

1. Boil together the sugar, water and lemon juice until quite thick.
2. Beat well.

You may also use the icing in the recipe above instead.

Makes 6 to 8 servings.

COOKIE SLICES
(Sausainiai)

1 cup butter
1½ cups sugar
6 eggs
7 cups flour
3 teaspoons baking powder
1 teaspoon vanilla
½ teaspoon cardamom seeds
1 cup nuts (walnuts, hazelnuts or pecans), chopped

Preheat oven to 400 degrees.

1. Cream the butter and sugar, then add the eggs one at a time. Beat well.
2. Sift in the flour and baking powder. Add the vanilla, cardamom seeds, and nuts.
3. Divide the dough into four sections. Shape each one into a long, round, thin loaf. Bake for about 30 minutes in a 400-degree oven. Remove from the pan.
4. While still warm, cut into ½-inch slices. Reduce the heat to 250 degrees. Place the slices on a cookie sheet and continue baking until they become dry and light brown.

Makes 40 to 50 cookies.

MUSHROOMS
(Grybai)

1 cup honey
½ cup sugar
4 tablespoons burnt sugar, caramelized in a pan
4 tablespoons butter
2 eggs
¼ cup sour cream
3½ cups flour
1½ teaspoons baking soda
1 tablespoon assorted spices (cinnamon, cloves, ginger,
    nutmeg, cardamom, grated lemon and orange rind)
Butter or shortening for greasing pans
Poppy seeds for decoration

Preheat oven to 350 degrees.

1. Heat the honey. Add the sugar, burnt sugar, butter, eggs
   and sour cream, alternately with flour and baking soda.
   Stir well.
2. Add the spices and knead until smooth. Divide the dough
   in half.
3. Form small pieces out of half the dough into various
   sized "mushroom caps," rounded on top, flat on the
   bottom, making an indentation with your fingertip in the
   flat side for insertion of the "stem". Place the flat side
   down on a greased cookie sheet.
4. Form stems by making several rolls of various thick-
   nesses to correspond to the mushroom caps, cut about
   1 to 1½ inches long. Wrap each stem in brown paper,
   leaving the ends open. Place on a greased cookie sheet,
   the overlapping side of the paper down.
5. Bake the caps and stems for 7 to 10 minutes. Cool.
6. Enlarge the mushroom cap indentation with a knife tip.
   Dip one end of the stem in the chocolate icing (recipe follows). Allow to set.

7. Ice flat side of caps and stems with white icing. Sprinkle several poppy seeds around the bottom of each stem. Ice mushroom tops with chocolate icing.

Icing:

2 cups sugar
½ cup water
½ tablespoon cold water for sprinkling
10 drops vinegar
2 teaspoons cocoa for chocolate part of the icing

1. Boil together the sugar and water until mixture becomes thick and bubbly. Remove from the heat and sprinkle with cold water.
2. Add vinegar. Cool. Beat until white. Divide icing in half. Add cocoa to one half for the chocolate icing.

Makes 10 to 12 "mushrooms," depending on size.

 ## FARINA PUDDING
(Manu Pudingas)

3 cups scalded milk
1 cup cold, cooked farina (cream of wheat)
2 eggs
½ cup sugar
¼ teaspoon salt
½ teaspoon vanilla
½ cup golden raisins
Butter for greasing pan

Preheat oven to 350 degrees.

1. Pour milk over farina. Add the eggs, sugar, salt, vanilla and raisins. Mix well.

2. Pour into a buttered baking dish. Bake until the pudding is firm (about 30 minutes).
3. Test by inserting a knife into the center. When it comes out clean, the pudding is done.

Serve with preserves.

Makes 3 to 4 servings.

 APPLE PIE

½ cup butter
5 tablespoons cream cheese
2 cups flour
2 tablespoons sugar
Zest of ½ lemon, grated
Butter and bread crumbs for spreading over baking pan
4 to 5 medium apples, peeled and cut fine
A bit of milk for brushing
1 tablespoon confectioners' sugar
2 tablespoons chopped walnuts

1. Mix butter and cream cheese together. Add the flour, sugar, and lemon zest, blend well, and place into the refrigerator overnight.
2. Divide the dough in two. Roll out one half and place into a baking dish, first greasing the bottom and sprinkling with bread crumbs.
3. Spread the apples over the dough, sprinkling with a little sugar if apples are tart. Cover with the remaining half of the dough. Cut several slits in the pie top for ventilation.
4. Brush the top of the pie with milk, then sprinkle with the confectioners' sugar and walnuts.
5. Bake at 350 degrees for 35 to 40 minutes.

Makes 5 to 6 servings.

CHERRIES "IN SHIRTS"

1 cup flour
¼ cup sugar, plus some for sprinkling
Cinnamon, to taste
2 eggs
1 cup white wine, heated
1½ pounds firm cherries, with stems
Butter for frying

1. Mix the flour, sugar, cinnamon, eggs and wine to form a loose dough.
2. Tie cherries into bunches of 6 to 8 by their stems with thread or string.
3. Dip the bunches into the batter and fry in hot butter on all sides until they are golden, shaking the pan often to prevent sticking.
4. Sprinkle sugar over the fried cherries.

Makes 5 to 6 servings.

 ## RICE WITH WHIPPED CREAM

3 cups milk
1 cup white rice
Dash of salt
½ cup sugar
¼ cup golden raisins
2 teaspoons vanilla, divided
2 cups fruit cocktail, drained
1 cup cream
2 teaspoons sugar
5 to 6 tablespoons raspberry preserves

1. Pour boiling milk over the rice. Add salt and sugar and cook over slow heat until the rice becomes soft (usually about 30 minutes).
2. Add the raisins and let them plump up in the hot rice mixture. Cool. Add 1 teaspoon of the vanilla and the fruit cocktail.
3. Whip the cream with the remaining vanilla and 2 teaspoons sugar.
4. Place the rice on the sides of a platter, making room for the cream to be piled into the middle.
5. Decorate the top of the rice roll with the preserves.

Makes 5 to 6 servings.

 STRAWBERRY MOUSSE

1 quart (4 cups) strawberries, hulled
½ cup confectioners' sugar
1 envelope gelatin
3 egg whites

1. Purée the strawberries and sugar through the blender until smooth.
2. Add the gelatin (dissolved in ½ cup of boiling water), blending again after this addition.
3. Whip the egg whites until stiff, and add the strawberry mixture gently.
4. Place into individual serving glasses or a platter when the mixture begins to gel and serve with plain waffle cookies.

Makes 4 to 5 servings.

BAKED RICE DESSERT

1 cup white rice
2½ cups milk
2 tablespoons butter
¾ cup sugar, divided
Pinch of salt
4 eggs, separated
2 tablespoons grated orange peel
1 tablespoon grated lemon peel
½ cup raisins
½ cup sour cream
1 tablespoon bread crumbs for lining pan

1. Cook the rice with milk over low heat, adding ½ cup of the sugar and a dash of salt, until it is soft and fluffy (about 20 to 25 minutes). Cool.

Preheat oven to 350 degrees.

2. Cream the egg yolks with the remaining sugar until light and fluffy and add to the rice.
3. Whip the egg whites until stiff and add to the rice mixture. Add the orange and lemon peel, the raisins, and the sour cream. Mix well.
4. Grease the pan with the remaining butter and sprinkle with bread crumbs.
5. Bake for about 30 minutes, or until it develops a golden top.

Serve with fruit syrup, such as currant or blueberry.

Makes 5 to 6 servings.

SEMI-CRISP MERINGUE PASTRY

For Pastry:

1 cup flour
6 tablespoons butter
¼ cup sugar
1 teaspoon vanilla
1 egg yolk
2½ tablespoons sour cream
1 teaspoon baking powder

For Topping and Meringue:

1 cup orange marmalade or other tart preserves
4 egg whites
⅛ teaspoon cream of tartar
¾ cup confectioners' sugar
½ teaspoon vanilla

1. Mix together the flour, butter, sugar, vanilla, egg yolk, sour cream, and baking powder. Work until smooth. Place in refrigerator to cool for 30 minutes.

Preheat oven to 350 degrees.

2. Roll out dough and place on a greased small cookie sheet. Pierce with a fork in several places before putting it into the oven.
3. Bake at 350 degrees for 25 to 30 minutes, or until lightly golden. Remove and cool slightly.

Reduce the oven temperature to 300 degrees.

4. Spread the jam or marmalade over the top of the pastry.
5. Whip the egg whites with the cream of tartar, sugar, and vanilla until they form stiff peaks. Spread over the pastry.

6. Bake in a 300-degree oven for 15 to 20 minutes, or until the meringue develops a slight blush.

Makes 5 to 6 servings.

 ## APPLE PAN CAKE

1 stick (¼ pound) butter, divided in half
2 eggs, separated
2 tablespoons sugar
2 cups flour
Peel of 1 lemon, grated
½ teaspoon salt
2 tablespoons bread crumbs
6 tart apples
4 tablespoons powdered sugar

1. Beat together ½ stick butter, egg yolks, and sugar.
2. Mix in flour (1 cup at a time) until batter is smooth. Add grated lemon peel and salt, and stir .
3. Fold in beaten egg whites and mix well.
4. Roll out dough. Divide in 2 parts. Transfer one part into greased frying pan (using remaining butter). Sprinkle with bread crumbs.
5. Slice cored apples. Sprinkle with sugar. Spread over dough.
6. Cover with the second rectangle of dough. Flip over and fry on other side. Sprinkle pan cake with powdered sugar.

Makes 4 to 5 servings.

DRINKS & COCKTAILS

BREAD CIDER
(Kvas)

Kvas may be served with many Lithuanian dishes, or as a refreshing summer drink.

1 gallon (16 cups) boiling water
2 pounds dried pumpernickel or dark rye bread
2½ cups sugar
2 tablespoons yeast
1 cup raisins

1. Pour boiling water over bread in a large pot. Let stand 5 hours.
2. Add sugar and bring to a boil. Cream yeast with a teaspoon each of sugar and water. Add to boiling mixture. Cool.
3. Skim off foam, pour into bottles, placing a handful of raisins in each bottle. Cork tightly.
4. Lay bottles on their sides in cool place. They are ready to drink in 2 to 3 days.

Makes about 4 one-quart bottles.

HONEY LIQUEUR
(Krupnikas)

1 teaspoon caraway seeds
10 cloves
10 whole allspice
2 to 3 cinnamon sticks
1 vanilla bean
2 one-inch pieces yellow ginger
2 one-inch pieces white ginger
10 cardamom seeds
½ nutmeg
Pinch of saffron
2 to 3 strips orange rind
2 to 3 strips lemon rind
4 cups water
2 pounds honey
1 quart grain alcohol(or strong plain vodka)
2 empty 1-quart bottles

1. Boil spices, rinds and water (first 13 ingredients) in covered pot until liquid is reduced to about 2 cups. Strain.
2. Bring honey to a boil separately, skimming off foam.
3. Pour first liquid into honey. Remove from heat.
4. Place far away from flame to prevent explosion of alcohol. Carefully and slowly pour in alcohol and replace pot on very low flame.
5. Heat slowly (do not simmer or boil) for 15 minutes. Remove from the fire and cool in same pot.
6. The next day, pour into bottles and allow to settle. If clearer liqueur is desired, filter through paper or cloth and rebottle.

Makes 2 one-quart bottles.

CRANBERRY CIDER

2 pounds cranberries
1 gallon boiling water
1 pound sugar
1 ounce yeast

1. Wash the cranberries. Place in a pot with cold water to cover. Boil until the berries pop.
2. Strain into a crock, pour on boiling water, and add sugar.
3. When lukewarm, add yeast dissolved in a little water. Cover, and place in a warm spot.
4. The next day, skim the top. Pour into bottles and cork. Keep in a cool place. The cider is ready to drink in 2 to 3 days.

Makes 4 one-quart bottles of cider.

 LEMON LIQUEUR

Rind of ½ lemon
2½ cups grain alcohol (or strong plain vodka)
4 unpeeled lemons
2 cups water
2 cups sugar

1. Soak the lemon rind in ½ cup of alcohol for 24 hours.
2. Wash and quarter the unpeeled lemons; add water, sugar, rind, and the alcohol in which rind is soaked.
3. Boil carefully for 15 minutes over medium heat. Cool and strain. Add the remaining 2 cups alcohol. Bottle.

Makes about one bottle (25.4 ounces) of liqueur.

MILK LIQUEUR

2 oranges
2 lemons
1 quart milk
1 quart grain alcohol (or strong plain vodka)
4 cups sugar
1 stick vanilla (or 2 teaspoons liquid vanilla)

1. Wash oranges and lemons. Cut into small pieces, leaving the peel on.
2. Combine milk, alcohol, and sugar. Add the vanilla stick, oranges, and lemons. Stir well.
3. Let stand for 3 weeks, stirring briskly every day.
4. Filter through filter paper or cotton and bottle.

Makes about 3 one-quart bottles.

INDEX

WIDENER UNIVERSITY
WOLFGRAM
LIBRARY
CHESTER, PA.

Other Cookbooks of Interest from HIPPOCRENE

Polish Heritage Cookery, Illustrated edition
Robert & Maria Strybel

New illustrated edition of a bestseller with 20 color photographs! Over 2,200 recipes in 29 categories, written especially for Americans!

"An encyclopedia of Polish Cookery and a wonderful thing to have!"
—*Julia Child, Good Morning America*

"*Polish Heritage Cookery* is the best [Polish] cookbook printed on the English market!"
—*Polish American Cultural Network*

915 pages • 16 pages color photographs • 0-7818-0558-9 • $39.95hc • (658)

The Best of Polish Cooking, Revised edition
Karen West

"A charming offering of Polish cuisine with lovely woodcuts throughout."
—*Publishers Weekly*

"Ethnic cuisine at it's best."
—*The Midwest Book Review*

219 pages • 0-87052-123-3 • $8.95pb • (391)

Old Warsaw Cookbook
Rysia

Includes 850 mouthwatering Polish recipes.
300 pages • 0-87052-932-3 • $12.95pb • (536)

Old Polish Traditions in the Kitchen and at the Table

A cookbook and history of Polish culinary customs. Short essays cover subjects like Polish hospitality, holiday traditions, even the exalted status of the mushroom. The recipes are traditional family fare.
304 pages • 0-7818-0488-4 • $11.95pb • (546)

ALL ALONG THE DANUBE

Recipes from Germany, Austria, Czechoslovakia, Yugoslavia, Hungary, Romania, and Bulgaria
Marina Polvay

For novices and gourmets, this unique cookbook offers a tempting variety of over 300 Central European recipes from the shores of the Danube River, bringing Old World flavor to today's dishes.
349 pages • 5½ x 8½ • numerous b/w photos & illustrations • 0-7818-0098-6 •W • $14.95pb • (491)

TASTE OF ROMANIA
Nicolae Klepper
"A brilliant cultural and culinary history . . . a collection of recipes to be treasured, tested and enjoyed."
—*George Lang, owner of Café des Artistes*

" . . . dishes like creamy cauliflower soup, sour cream-enriched *mamaliga* (the Romanian polenta), lamb stewed in sauerkraut juice and scallions, and *mititei* (exactly like the ones I tasted so long ago in Bucharest) are simple and appealing . . . Klepper paints a pretty picture of his native country's culinary possibilities."
—*Colman Andrews, Saveur magazine*
A real taste of both Old World and modern Romanian culture. More than 140 recipes, including the specialty dishes of Romania's top chefs, are intermingled with fables, poetry, photos and illustrations in this comprehensive and well-organized guide to Romanian cuisine.
319 pages • 5½ x 8½ • photos/illustrations • 0-7818-0523-6 •W • $24.95hc • (637)

TRADITIONAL BULGARIAN COOKING
Atanas Slavov
This collection of over 125 authentic recipes, the first comprehensive Bulgarian cookbook published in English, spans the range of home cooking: including many stews and hearty soups using lamb or poultry and grilled meats, vegetables and cheese pastries; deserts of sweetmeats rich in sugar and honey, puddings, and dried fruit compotes.
200 pages • 5½ x 8½ • 0-7818-0581-3 •W • $22.50hc • (681)

THE BEST OF CZECH COOKING
Peter Trnka
Over 200 simple yet elegant recipes from this little-known cuisine.
248 pages • 5 x 8½ • 0-7818-0492-2 •W • $12.95pb • (376)

THE ART OF HUNGARIAN COOKING, Revised edition
Paul Pogany Bennett and Velma R. Clark
Whether you crave Chicken Paprika or Apple Strudel, these 222 authentic Hungarian recipes inlude a vast array of national favorites, from appetizers through desserts. Now updated with a concise guide to Hungarian wines!
225 pages • 5½ x 8½ • 18 b/w drawings • 0-7818-0586-4 •W • $11.95pb • (686)

BEST OF AUSTRIAN CUISINE

Elisabeth Mayer-Browne

Nearly 200 recipes from Austria's rich cuisine: roasted meats in cream sauces, hearty soups and stews, tasty dumplings, and, of course, the pastries and cakes that remain Vienna's trademark.

224 pages • 5 x 8½ • 0-7818-0526-0 •W • $11.95pb • (633)

A BELGIAN COOKBOOK

Juliette Elkon

A celebration of the regional variations found in Belgian cuisine.

224 pages • 5½ x 8½ • 0-7818-0461-2 •W • $12.95pb • (535)

CELTIC COOKBOOK: Traditional Recipes from the Six Celtic Lands Brittany, Cornwall, Ireland, Isle of Man, Scotland and Wales

Helen Smith-Twiddy

This collection of over 160 recipes from the Celtic world includes traditional, yet still popular dishes like Rabbit Hoggan and Gwydd y Dolig (Stuffed Goose in Red Wine).

200 pages • 5½ x 8½ • 0-7818-0579-1 • NA • $22.50hc • (679)

TRADITIONAL RECIPES FROM OLD ENGLAND

Arranged by country, this charming classic features the favorite dishes and mealtime customs from across England, Scotland, Wales and Ireland.

128 pages • 5 x 8½ • 0-7818-0489-2 •W • $9.95pb • (157)

THE ART OF IRISH COOKING

Monica Sheridan

Nearly 200 recipes for traditional Irish fare.

166 pages • 5½ x 8½ • 0-7818-0454-X •W • $12.95pb • (335)

ART OF DUTCH COOKING

C. Countess van Limburg Stirum

This attractive volume of 200 recipes offers a complete cross section of Dutch home cooking, adapted to American kitchens. A whole chapter is devoted to the Dutch Christmas, with recipes for unique cookies and candies that are a traditional part of the festivities.

192 pages • 5½ x 8½ • illustrations • 0-7818-0582-1 •W • $11.95pb •(683)

TRADITIONAL FOOD FROM SCOTLAND: THE EDINBURGH BOOK OF PLAIN COOKERY RECIPES

A delightful assortment of Scottish recipes and helpful hints for the home—this classic volume offers a window into another era.

336 pages • 5½ x 8 • 0-7818-0514-7 •W • $11.95pb • (620)

TRADITIONAL FOOD FROM WALES

Bobby Freeman

Welsh food and customs through the centuries. This book combines over 260 authentic, proven recipes with cultural and social history

332 pages • 5½ x 8½ • 0-7818-0527-9 • NA • $24.95 • (638)

BEST OF SCANDINAVIAN COOKING: DANISH, NORWEGIAN AND SWEDISH

Shirley Sarvis and Barbara Scott O'Neil

This exciting collection of 100 recipes, each dish the favorite of a Scandinavian cook, spans the range of home cooking, appetizers, soups, omelets, pancakes, meats and pastries.

142 pages • 5 x 8½ • 0-7818-0547-3 •W • $9.95pb • (643)

THE BEST OF FINNISH COOKING

Taimi Previdi

Two hundred easy to follow recipes covering all courses of the meal, along with menu suggestions and cultural background for major holidays and festivities such as Mayday and Midsummer.

242 pages • 5 x 8½ • Bilingual index • 0-7818-0493-0 •W • $12.95pb • (601)

THE ART OF TURKISH COOKING

Nesret Eren

"Her recipes are utterly mouthwatering, and I cannot remember a time when a book so inspired me to take pot in hand."

—*Nika Hazelton, The New York Times Book Review*

308 pages • 5½ x 8½ • 0-7818-0201-6 •W • $12.95pb • (162)